Teaching Reading Essentials:

Video Demonstrations of Small-Group Interventions

Program Guide

Louisa Moats
Linda Farrell

11 10 09 08 07   2 3 4 5 6

ISBN 1-59318-730-0

Printed in the United States of America

Published and distributed by

Sopris West™
EDUCATIONAL SERVICES

A Cambium Learning Company

4093 Specialty Place • Longmont, Colorado 80504
(303) 651-2829 • www.sopriswest.com

[146499/10-06]

Acknowledgements

Funding for the development of *Teaching Reading Essentials*, originally entitled *Colleague in the Classroom*, was awarded by the National Institute of Child Health and Human Development's (NICHD's) Small Business Innovation Research Program through grant #HD042376-02 to Sopris West Educational Services.

A team of diligent researchers managed this project from its inception. Stu Horsfall committed the company's resources and expertise to this project. Jodie Simon was instrumental in obtaining the original grant, while Christine Willis and Judith McCabe directed and administered the research program with exemplary professionalism. Janel Dalglish assisted the research team in data collection and management of myriad details.

Michelle LaBorde smoothly guided the development of *Teaching Reading Essentials* from planning to production. Sarah Beatty's team produced and edited hours of high-quality demonstration video. Rob Carson oversaw the editing of this *Program Guide*. Many thanks to all in the production, editing, and design departments who had a hand in the final product.

Tina Osenga wrote major portions of the original manual for *Colleague in the Classroom.* Mary Ellen Cummings contributed her teaching expertise for the original product as well.

Barbara Wise and Anne Whitney provided expert consultation during the development of the new version, and Anne Whitney contributed talking points for each demonstration.

We are indebted to the children, teachers, and administrators at two Colorado schools, Pleasant View Elementary in Golden and Annunciation School in Denver, who contributed their time and resources, tolerated inconveniences, and collaborated with us to support both *Colleague in the Classroom* and *Teaching Reading Essentials.*

Meet the Authors

Louisa Moats, Ed.D., is well known for her publications on reading instruction, the professional development of teachers, and the relationship between language, reading, and spelling. She has published in many peer-reviewed journals and written numerous books and book chapters. Louisa authored the American Federation of Teachers' *Teaching Reading Is Rocket Science,* Learning First Alliance's *Every Child Reading: A Professional Development Guide,* and The Reading First Leadership Academy's *Professional Development Blueprint.* Her professional development program, *Language Essentials for Teachers of Reading and Spelling* (LETRS), with which the lessons in *Teaching Reading Essentials* are aligned, evolved from Dr. Moats' many years of experience teaching classroom teachers and reading specialists in graduate programs and in school systems.

Linda Farrell, MBA., is a partner and reading specialist with the Really Great Reading Company. She provides professional development for educators around the country. In addition, she develops products for beginning and struggling readers. Linda designed the letter tiles used in the *Teaching Reading Essentials* videos. She also developed the Beginning and Advanced Decoding Surveys included in LETRS and in this *Program Guide.*

Linda is a National LETRS Trainer for Sopris West and co-author of *DIBELS: A Practical Manual* (Sopris West, 2006). She received a Volunteer of the Year award in the District of Columbia for her efforts in the field of adult literacy.

Meet the Teachers

Carolyn Denton, Ph.D., is an assistant professor in the Department of Special Education at the University of Texas at Austin and serves on the board of directors of the Vaughn Gross Center for Reading and Language Arts at the University of Texas.

Judi Dodson, M.A., is a literacy consultant who is developing curriculum and training teachers for Colorado Reading First. Judi is a National LETRS Trainer.

Holly Graves is the president of a private clinic for individuals with dyslexia and related challenges. Holly provides teacher training and consultation to private and public schools in the Denver area.

Michael Hunter, a partner in Really Great Reading Company, gives workshops nationally and develops assessments, intervention lessons, phonics instruction, and multi-sensory manipulative materials to help beginning and struggling readers. He works with struggling readers of all ages whenever he finds time.

Elizabeth Ramos is a bilingual teacher who works with early elementary school students and specializes in providing targeted reading interventions in both English and Spanish.

Meet the Students

Students participating in *Teaching Reading Essentials* were recruited from kindergarten through third grade classrooms in an urban school serving 85 % Hispanic and 15 % African-American students and other ethnicities. Approximately 75 % of the student body is eligible for free and reduced lunch. Instruction in the school is English only, although some students are English Language Learners (ELLs), some are bilingual, and some are from monolingual English-speaking households. All but the kindergarten students had received one to three years of instruction in English prior to the time the *Teaching Reading Essentials* lessons were videotaped. Students participating in *Teaching Reading Essentials* lessons had been screened prior to formation of the groups to determine their instructional needs. The screening instruments used were the *Dynamic Indicators of Basic Early Literacy Skills* (DIBELS) and brief informal diagnostic assessments such as the Informal Reading Surveys included in Appendix J.

The video demonstrations you see in *Teaching Reading Essentials* are authentic interactions between teachers and students. They were not rehearsed, redone, or doctored. You will see that, in many instances, students and teachers were just getting to know one another.

Meet the Participants

Special thanks to the thirty-two early reading educators featured in the professional development sessions with Dr. Moats.

These teachers represent a variety of backgrounds and experience, ranging from two to more than thirty years in the classroom. Currently, they work in the Jefferson County School District in Colorado, which serves more than 85,000 children. They brought a wealth of knowledge and wisdom to the conversations about the *Teaching Reading Essentials* demonstration videos. We hope their comments and their professionalism will serve as a model for your own professional development meetings.

Table of Contents

Part 3: Teaching Beginning Reading and Writing 53

Welcome to *Teaching Reading Essentials*

What is *Teaching Reading Essentials?*

Teaching Reading Essentials is a professional development program for teachers of beginning reading and writing skills. It is not a reading program for students, although the demonstrations show instructional techniques that are aligned with or central to existing research-based reading and writing intervention programs.

Teaching Reading Essentials provides 58 video demonstrations of small-group instruction modeled by expert teachers. The video demonstrations are organized by areas of instruction based on research-driven models of reading development. Demonstrations run between 3 minutes and 34 minutes in length, and total approximately 12 hours of material.

Teaching Reading Essentials is delivered in a set of five DVDs. The teaching demonstrations are accompanied by this *Program Guide*, which contains a short written description of each demonstration, talking points for viewers, and links to instructional programs that contain those techniques.

Teaching Reading Essentials DVDs also include introductions by Dr. Moats and discussions Dr. Moats conducted with teachers after they viewed some of the videos during professional development sessions.

How should *Teaching Reading Essentials* be used?

Teaching Reading Essentials can be used for various purposes:

- By reading coaches at team meetings.
- By individual teachers who want to study the expert modeling of instructional techniques in the lessons.
- By mentor teachers who are training tutors or paraprofessionals.
- By professional development providers to add demonstrations to their presentations.

Those using *Teaching Reading Essentials* should be aware that many techniques and activities demonstrated with small groups in the lessons can also be incorporated into whole-class instruction. Talking points to guide discussions are included with each demonstration.

How is *Teaching Reading Essentials* aligned with existing professional development programs and screening instruments?

LETRS. *Teaching Reading Essentials* is fully aligned with the content of the *Language Essentials for Teachers of Reading and Spelling* (LETRS) (Sopris West, 2005) professional development modules and may be used as an adjunct to LETRS. (For more information about LETRS, see Appendix C.)

DIBELS. The demonstrations in *Teaching Reading Essentials* are indexed explicitly to the *Dynamic Indicators of Basic Early Literacy Skills* (DIBELS) indicators. If you know a student's DIBELS results, you can immediately focus on the *Teaching Reading Essentials* instructional strategies that are appropriate for the student.

Other Early Screening Instruments. The demonstrations align well with other valid screening instruments, such as the *Texas Primary Reading Inventory* (TPRI), the *Predictive Assessment of Reading* (PAR), and *Phonological Awareness Literacy Screening* (PALS) from the University of Virginia.

Where can I find programs that include the demonstrated lessons?

Many demonstrated activities can be found in Carolyn Denton and Jennifer Hocker's validated intervention program, *Responsive Reading Instruction: Flexible Intervention for Struggling Readers in the Early Grades* (Sopris West, 2006), and in Linda Farrell and Michael Hunter's intervention program, *Targeted Reading Lessons* (Really Great Reading Company, 2007). Other compatible programs published by Sopris West Educational Services include *WatchWord* (2005), *Spelling by Pattern* (2007); *Phonics and Spelling Through Phoneme-Grapheme Mapping* (2006), and the PALS series (2001). Demonstrated techniques and activites are also parts of various multisensory structured language programs and core, comprehensive instructional programs with systematic, explicit phonology and phonics components.

Navigating through the *Teaching Reading Essentials* DVDs

This "How To" page is designed to help you understand the *Teaching Reading Essentials* format and how best to put the guide and DVDs to work for you.

Step 1: Choose a Part to Review

Begin by choosing a part to review. The parts are:

Part 1: Teaching Letters, Sounds, and Sense (Disk 1)

Phonological Awareness
Letter Knowledge
Concepts of Print

Part 2: Teaching Phoneme Awareness (Disk 2)

Single Phonemes
Segmentation and Blending

Part 3: Teaching Beginning Reading and Writing (Disks 3a and 3b)

Disk 3A

Basic Routines
A Complete Lesson on Short *i* Words
Teaching Spelling Patterns

Disk 3B

Fluency and Comprehension – Decodable Text
Fluency and Comprehension – Leveled Text
Supported Writing
Comprehensive, Integrated Lesson

Part 4: Teaching Advanced Phonics (Disk 4)

Introducing Critical Concepts
Vowel-Consonant-*e*
More Syllable Patterns
Multiple Spellings for a Long Vowel

Part 5: Teaching Vocabulary and Comprehension (Disk 5)

Word Meaning Activities
Integrated Lessons

Next, select and insert the DVD featuring the part you'd like to review into your DVD player or computer.

Note: Part 3 is delivered on two DVDs, 3A and 3B.

When using a DVD player:

1. Insert the DVD into the DVD player. The DVD will play automatically.
2. Use the arrow keys on your DVD remote to make a selection on the menu, then hit Enter. At any time during a segment you can hit the Menu button on your remote to return to the DVD menu.
3. At the end of each segment you will be automatically returned to the DVD menu.

When using a computer:

1. Check with the manufacturer to make sure your computer supports DVD playback.
2. Insert DVD into DVD player. The DVD will load automatically.
3. If the DVD doesn't appear within a full screen, select Video (Mac) or View (PC) at the top, then click Full Screen. Controls differ with varying programs.
4. Use your mouse or arrow keys to make a selection, then click or hit ENTER to play the selection.

Step 2: Watch the Introduction by Louisa Moats

Watch the video Introduction by Louisa Moats for each part.

Step 3: Watch the Demonstrations

Now you're ready to watch the demonstrations. Click on the demonstration you'd like to watch.

Many demonstrations are accompanied by a video of a professional development session that discusses the content of the corresponding demonstration. The professional development sessions provide a model for how schools and coaches can use the demonstrations in their own training scenarios.

Step 4: Refer to This Program Guide

All the demonstrations featured on the *Teaching Reading Essentials DVDs* are described in detail in this program guide. Lists of materials and instructional procedures have been carefully outlined to support the use of these activities in your own classroom. There are also discussion points included to guide and enhance the staff development experience for you and your colleagues.

Part 1—Teaching Letters, Sounds, and Sense

What is involved in the task of reading?

Reading is much more than being able to look at letters and read a word. Proficient readers use several language processing systems to get meaning from reading. All of the processing systems must work together to support reading, and all must be educated.

- **Syntactic processing** requires knowledge of sentence patterns.
- **Semantic processing** (vocabulary) supports understanding of word meaning.
- **Orthographic processing** enables us to recognize and remember letter sequences.
- **Phonological processing** involves awareness of our speech sound system.

In addition to these systems, good readers have developed **discourse pragmatics**, which is knowledge of how we use language socially and contextually to communicate ideas.

What is phonological awareness?

In Part 1 of *Teaching Reading Essentials*, several lessons demonstrate how to teach students about sounds in words and sentences. These lessons address **phonological awareness**, which is a student's ability to identify, think about, and manipulate parts of spoken words. Phonological awareness is part of **word consciousness** or **metalinguistic awareness**.

There are four parts of spoken language that students need to be able to identify, think about, and manipulate in order to demonstrate phonological awareness. These parts can be arranged in a hierarchy from easiest to most difficult:

- **Words**—For example, students need to understand that "the dog" is two words, not one. This skill is usually learned in preschool or kindergarten.
- **Syllables**—Students need to be able to orally segment and blend spoken syllables. This skill is often learned in preschool or kindergarten.

- **Onset and rime**—Understanding that words have onset and rime is the foundation of a student's ability to rhyme. Rhyming requires a student to change a word's onset but leave the rime the same. Many students master rhyming in preschool or kindergarten. (**Onset** is the part of the syllable before the vowel. **Rime** is the part of the syllable that includes the vowel. In the word *blast, bl* is the onset, and *ast* is the rime. Not all words have an onset. *At, end,* and *eye* are examples of words without an onset.)
- **Phonemes**—Students need to hear phonemes, the smallest units of sound in a word, before they can match them to letters when they read and spell. Phoneme awareness, the most difficult level of phonological awareness, is generally mastered by the end of kindergarten by students who are progressing well in learning to read. Students who have not mastered phoneme awareness by the end of kindergarten may need specific instruction in this area in order to become proficient readers.

What is phonological processing?

Phonological processing is an umbrella term for dimensions of language processing that have to do with knowledge of our speech sound system. Phonological processing includes:

- The production and pronunciation of words.
- Memory for the sounds of spoken language.
- The ability to recognize words as belonging to one's own language system.
- The ability to supply prosody or phrasing to spoken language.
- The ability to detect which speech sounds are in words.

When we use the term *phonological processing* in early reading instruction, we include not only phonological awareness but also accurate memory for word pronunciation.

What is a phoneme?

A **phoneme** is the smallest unit of speech that determines word meaning. For example, the words *cloud* and *clown* differ in one phoneme (the final consonant). The words *etymology* and *entymology* differ in one phoneme (*entymology* has one extra phoneme, which is an /n/).

Phonemes are the building blocks of spoken words; they must be identified, separated, and blended by anyone who is learning to read and write with an alphabet. They also must be perceived and remembered as we learn new vocabulary words.

Phonemes can be divided into **vowels** and **consonants**, terms that describe sounds as well as letters. Vowels are sounds that are voiced and have no obstruction when produced. Vowels are the heart of a syllable, and every syllable must have a vowel sound. Consonants can be voiced or unvoiced, and they have some type of obstruction when produced. The English language has about 18 vowel sounds and 25 consonant sounds that are spelled with only 26 letters and their combinations.

Who needs phonological awareness instruction?

Instruction at this level is for students who are at the beginning stages of reading or who may be struggling learning to read and exhibit one or more of the following traits:

- Score below benchmark on DIBELS Letter Naming Fluency (LNF) and Initial Sound Fluency (ISF).
- Do not "tune in" to or attend carefully to the sounds of language and who need to develop linguistic awareness.
- Are not aware that words can be broken into sound segments such as onset and rime or syllables, and therefore are not ready for phonemic awareness instruction.
- Cannot recognize or produce rhyme.
- May not know the terms *word, syllable, rhyme, letter,* or *first, second, third, last.*
- Have limited experience with books and how they are read.
- Are English Language Learners (ELLs) or learners with limited English proficiency.

Why should we teach basic phonological skills?

Beginning readers need to have phonemic awareness because part of the reading process involves matching phonemes (sounds) with graphemes (letters). Students who have not developed phonemic awareness cannot understand letter-sound relationships. We know from scientific studies that 80 % –90 % of students with reading difficulties need help with phonemic awareness. However, some children are not ready to focus on phonemes because they are too difficult. When children struggle with phonemic awareness concepts, they may need to back up and learn to "tune in" to larger segments of speech, such as onset and rime or syllables.

Screening and diagnostic assessments often begin with phoneme segmentation and blending tasks because children must achieve phonemic awareness in order to be able to read. Children who are not good at isolating speech sounds in words may first need to attend to and differentiate larger segments of speech. Progressive differentiation of larger to smaller units of speech can follow a path from words in sentences, to syllables, to onset and rime segments, and then to phonemes.

The goal of phonological instruction is to enable children to remember, retrieve, and think about all the sounds in words—or what researchers call a "fully specified internal image" of a word. We want children to automatically and accurately think about the sound structure of words, including syllables, onset and rime, and phonemes. This ability to easily relate to spoken word parts allows them to connect sound easily so they can concentrate on meaning and use when they read.

Phonological instruction focuses on *spoken,* not *written,* language in the beginning stages because many students need practice directing their attention to speech. Letters and print can be brought into lessons and matched to speech sounds as soon as students have demonstrated that they are primed to focus on speech.

Many young children and older poor readers benefit from instruction in phonological awareness that progresses gradually from syllable awareness to phoneme awareness. Unstructured or playful experiences with language coupled with direct, explicit teaching can be helpful in building phonological skills for students of any age.

What should we teach to students who need to learn phonological awareness?

Sounds, letters, and meaning. A beginning reading lesson may include parallel but separate strands of "listening" and phonological awareness, letter knowledge, language development, and concepts of print. As each foundation strand is strengthened, the strands can be linked with each other. For example, sounds and letters can be connected much more efficiently once the foundational phonological and letter recognition skills are established separately than if teachers attempt to match letters and sounds before a student has demonstrated phonological awareness.

Word awareness. Students who are learning to read must have basic awareness that sentences and phrases are composed of words that have phonological boundaries. In our demonstrations, print-speech correspondence at the word level is taught with a print tracking activity (Demonstration 9). Word awareness can also be taught with colored felt squares that stand for words.

Syllable awareness. Words can be broken into syllables (Demonstrations 2 and 3). The easiest syllables for students to grasp are two-syllable compound words because each syllable can stand alone. For example, the word *cupcake* splits into the words *cup* and *cake*. Students then identify syllables in non-compound words (e.g., *table* splits into *ta-ble*). Students are asked to identify, blend, segment, and substitute syllables with the aid of colored felt squares.

Onset and rime facility. Single syllables can be broken into onset and rime (Demonstrations 4 and 5). Onset includes all sounds before the vowel sound in the syllable and rime includes the vowel and all sounds that follow. For example, the word *street* has the onset */str/* and the rime */eet/*. When students understand these parts, they can understand that rhyming words have the same rime. When students have difficulty with identifying or producing rhymes, it is because they do not understand that syllables can be broken into these parts.

When do we teach letters and concepts of print?

Knowledge of letters. At the same time language development and phonological awareness are taught, children need to learn the letter forms, letter names, and letter sequence in the alphabet (Demonstrations 6, 7, and 8). Research demonstrates that the ability to accurately name letters is one of the best single predictors of later success in reading. Lots of daily practice with manipulatives and many multisensory activities can support development of letter knowledge. A goal for young children is fluent letter naming, achieved through ample, varied practice with letter matching, sequencing, writing, and naming. Once phonological awareness is demonstrated and letters can be identified, matched, named, and copied, children are ready for letter-sound matching and reading itself.

Concepts of print and vocabulary of instruction. Many children come to school without experience with books. Print awareness activities are designed to teach students about the format of books, conventions such as left-to-right progression and the significance of spaces between words, and the expectation that the words should make sense. Many children must be taught the language of instruction, including the names for language parts (e.g., word, letter, sentence) and position words such as first, second, and third and beginning and ending.

DVD Navigation

Part 1: Teaching Letters, Sounds, and Sense			
For students who are below benchmark on DIBELS ISF and LNF.			
Demonstration Video	**Activity Name**	**Page**	**Time (minutes)**
	Introduction to Part 1		29:49
Phonological Awareness			
1	Bilingual Scaffolding	10	4:21
2	Syllable Blending	11	4:09
3	Syllable Substitution	12	2:41
4	Onset and Rime Professional Development Session	13	4:53 6:46
5	Producing Rhyming Words Professional Development Session	15	5:03 8:25
Letter Knowledge			
6	Alphabet Sequence	17	4:51
7	Letter Naming	18	3:03
8	Letter Formation Professional Development Session	19	4:52 10:18
Concepts of Print			
9	Print-Related Vocabulary Professional Development Session	21	10:50 6:12
10	One-to-One Correspondence	24	10:17
11	Does It Make Sense?	27	8:10

Bilingual Scaffolding

Elizabeth uses Spanish to clarify the task for a new kindergarten student with limited English. She instructs in English, but rephrases in both languages, providing enough scaffolding for the student to understand and participate.

Lesson Component:
Awareness of sounds.

Objective:
Students will learn a key word /beginning with a target speech sound.

Materials:
Various props (e.g., an apple for /ă/

Instructional Procedure:
- Stretch out the speech sound as you pair it with a gesture.
- Ask students to imitate the sound and the gesture.
- Play a recognition game with students: If you make the gesture, then students make the sound. If you make the sound, then students make the sound and the gesture.

Talking Points for Professional Development:
" Note how easily the teacher switched languages to ensure that both English and Spanish speaking students understood directions. What if you are monolingual English?

▶ Note the animation and exaggeration of facial features and expression.

▶ Note the ample practice time—every student got a turn.

▶ Because the movement rather than the sound-symbol correspondence became the focus, the teacher could have restated the name and sound of the letter.

Syllable Blending

Syllable blending follows simple syllable counting activities such as those described in the introductory video to this section. For example, *macaroni* has four syllables, *ma-ca-ro-ni*, that you can say while tapping the table with the side of your fist, sweeping left to right (from the students' perspective) while blending the syllables together to say the word.

Other techniques for syllable awareness: Ask students to say the word loudly while holding their lips together ("Duck Lips") to feel each syllable's vocalization, or ask students to put their hands under their chins and look in the mirror to see and feel their jaw drop on each syllable.

Lesson Component:

Phonological awareness (syllables).

Objective:

Students will blend words with two to four syllables.

Materials:

- Lists of words with two to four syllables.
- Magnetized colored felt squares (five of one color) and a magnetic white board.

Instructional Procedure—Blending a Word by Syllables:

- Say, *I'm going to say a word by its parts. Can you guess the word? Think, but don't say it. Mo-tor-cy-cle. Now you say it fast.* (Motorcycle!)
- Guide group practice, saying each word slowly by syllables. Say, *Listen and think. Cer-e-al. Now say it fast.* (Cereal.)
- Call on individual students to name the word you have broken into parts.
- Add interest and meaning by using students' names, or words from a unit of study or story students have heard.
- Use colored squares to represent the separate syllables. Say the syllables of a word, putting squares on the table; then, push the squares together as you blend the word.

Talking Points for Professional Development:

▸ How effective is the reinforcement?

▸ Notice the repetition.

▸ What if Michael had stated "why" before he started and concluded with "what was learned"?

▸ How effective is the teacher's pause time? If he changed the length of the pause, what might happen?

Syllable Substitution

Once students can blend, segment, add, and delete syllables in spoken words, they are ready to substitute syllables. Colored squares can represent syllables. Explicitly teaching students to show syllable changes with squares prepares them for the more difficult task of showing phonemic changes.

Lesson Component:
Phonological awareness (syllables).

Objective:
Students will substitute syllables in spoken words.

Materials:
- Lists of words with syllable changes.

| ta/per | ta/ble | mar/ble | mar/ket | bas/ket | bas/ket/ry |

- Magnetized colored felt squares (five of one color) and a magnetic white board.
- Sets of colored squares (four colors) for each student.

Instructional Procedure:

I DO
- Say, *We're going to change one syllable at a time to make new words. We'll use the colored squares to show the changes. Watch me first. This square stands for /tā/. Let's make the word* **taper.** *Taper is a candle. We'll add another square to /tā/ to show that we've added the syllable /**per**/. What's the word?*
- *Now, I'll change something. We have* **ta-per** *(touch and say). Let's make it* **table.** *Which part will change? Yes, the last syllable changed, so we need to change the second square.*

WE DO
- Say, *Let's change* **table** *to* **marble** *(touch and say). What part changes? Yes, the first syllable changed, so we'll change the first square.*
- Lead the group to make additional changes.

YOU DO
- Give each student a turn to change a syllable and explain what he or she changed.

Talking Points for Professional Development:
▶ Notice the use of "I do, We do, You do" during the lesson.
▶ What is the advantage of using a word like *awesome*?

Onset and Rime

Production of a rhyming word is problematic for many students. They benefit from direct teaching about the two parts of a syllable, onset and rime, and practice blending, segmenting, and making changes in those parts. The stage is then set for direct teaching of the concept of rhyming.

Lesson Component:
Phonological awareness (onset and rime).

Objective:
Students will identify and blend the onset and rime parts of a syllable, and substitute onsets to make new words.

Materials:
- Lists of one-syllable words.
- Colored felt squares. Felt boards or magnetic white boards.

Instructional Procedure—Blending a Word by Onset and Rime:

I DO
- Say, *I'm going to say a syllable in two parts. Can you name the word? Think, but don't say it. S – ock. Say it fast. Sock!* (Alternative signal: Turn over one hand at a time as onset and rime are spoken, then bring hands together for the whole word.)

WE DO
- Guide group practice, saying each word slowly by onset and rime. Say, *Listen and think. Ch-air. Now say it fast. Chair.*

YOU DO
- Call on individuals to say the parts and move their hands together as they say the word fast.

Scaffolding:
- Words without initial consonant blends are easiest (dawn; rode; think).
- Words students know the meaning of are easiest.
- Students' names and words from a unit of study or story students have heard add interest.

Instructional Procedure—Substituting Onsets:

Introduce representing onset and rime with felts or colored tiles.

I DO
- Say a word. Place two colored squares on the magnet board as you say the onset and rime parts of a one-syllable word. Point to the corresponding square as you say each word part. Run your finger under the two parts and say the word.

/m/	/ăt/

- Pass out a set of colored squares to each student.

WE DO
- Ask students to place two colored squares on their desks. They will need these to match the onset and rime as you demonstrate.
- Say a word. Say the onset and rime as you touch each square. Ask students to touch each square as they say the onset and rime, then run their finger under the squares and say the word.
- Touch and say the onset-rime parts of several more words as students copy your movements with their own squares. Point to either the onset or rime and ask, *What does this part say?*

/p/	/art/		/tr/	/ain/

/ch/	/ild/		/g/	/ood/

YOU DO
- After guided practice, give individual students two parts of a word and ask each student to touch and say which part, then blend the parts into a word.

Substituting Onsets

I DO
- Say, *I'm going to change this part of* **child** *to make a new word. If I change* /ch/ *to* /w/ [change the color of the onset as you say the new sound(s)], *I will have* **wild**. *I changed* **child** *to* **wild** *by changing the first part and keeping the last part the same.*

WE DO
- Continue giving guided practice.

YOU DO
- After you have guided the practice, ask students to think of a way the first part (onset) could change to make a new word with the last part. If they make a nonsense word, accept it but say that the word is a nonsense word—not a real word.
- Finally, say, *When the last parts sound the same, the words are rhyming words.*

Talking Points for Professional Development:

▸ What happens with the "teachable moment"? Is this a consistent pattern? If so, what can you do?

▸ Notice that the teacher gives the student the first sound (part or onset) and asks him to produce the second part. Why is that a good introductory method?

Producing Rhyming Words

Production of rhyme depends on whether students recognize that the rimes of two or more words are the same. Again, rimes are the vowel sound and the sounds that follow the vowel in a syllable.

Lesson Component:
Phonological awareness.

Objective:
Students will produce a rhyme by changing the onset in a syllable.

Materials:
- Colored felt squares with magnetic backing and a white board.
- Pictures of several objects with one-syllable names that rhyme (*coat, boat, float, goat; knee, tree, bee; mouse, house, grouse; ship, zip, trip, clip*).

Instructional Procedure—Identifying the Rhyming Part:

I DO

- Say, "*Hickory Dickory dock, the mouse ran up the clock.*" *Which words rhyme?* (dock and clock) *I'll show you why they rhyme.*
- *Dock has two parts, /d/ and /ŏck/.* (Put two different colored felt squares on the board. Point to them as you explain.) *This part is /d/. This part is /ŏck/. What part is this?* (/ock/) *What part is this?* (/d/) *What's the word?* (dock)
- *When we make a rhyming word, we keep this part the same* (point to the rime square), *and we change the first part.* (Change the color of the first square as new rhyming words are made.) *Watch me. If I change **dock** to **clock**, I change the first part but keep the last part the same. Now let's change **clock** to **sock**. What part do I change?*

YOU DO

- Ask students to change the color of the first or last square as you say *sock, shock, shack,* and *stack*.

WE DO

- With students, change the color of the first or last square as you say several words: *luck, lack, back, sack, tack, tick*.

Instructional Procedure—Producing Rhyming Words:

I DO

- Place two squares of different colors on the white board. Say, *These two squares show the parts of* **house,** */h/ /ouse/. Let's make some rhyming words. I'll make the first one. I'll change /h/ to /m/ and keep /ouse/ the same* **(mouse)**.

/h/	/ouse/

/m/	/ouse/

WE DO

- With students, touch and say the squares as they repeat and blend the onset and rime.

YOU DO

- Ask students to name a picture and show the two parts of the word (onset and rime) with their colored squares.

- Next, ask students to find another picture with a name that rhymes with the first. Ask students to show with the squares how the first part of the word changed. The last part stayed the same, so the color of the square stayed the same.

- Repeat the exercise with different rhyming words. Every three or four items, ask students to change the rime part (e.g., change the /ell/ in **well** to /all/). Ask, *If I change this part, will the words rhyme?* (No.) *Correct. The end part has to stay the same for the words to rhyme.*

Talking Points for Professional Development:

▶ Note the physical/visual differences between the rectangles for onsets and rimes. Why is it important to have different sizes and colors?

▶ How does the teacher scaffold instruction?

▶ If students can't perform this task, what should we teach them?

Alphabet Sequence

Learning the alphabet letter names can be accomplished with games and manipulative activities, such as matching letter forms to the template on an alphabet arc.

Lesson Component:
Letter knowledge.

Objective:
With group support, students will match the letter shapes, recognize them by name, and say the alphabet in order, while pointing to the letters in an array.

Materials:
- Alphabet arcs or mats.
- Uppercase and lowercase sets of plastic letters.

Instructional Procedure—Naming the Alphabet in Sequence:
- Give each student an alphabet arc and set of letter shapes. (Uppercase is often learned first.)
- Select some letters for students to match and hand them out.
- Ask each student to match the plastic letters to the shape outlines on the arc.
- (More advanced.) Ask students to match the shapes in order, from A to Z, then backwards, from Z to A.
- With students, sing the alphabet song while everybody points to the letters in order.
- Say "chunks" of the array while pointing to the letters, asking students to say the sequence with you, then ask students to say the sequence as you point. (For example, ABCDEFG—HIJKLMN—OPQRSTU—VWXYZ.)
- Say the letter names randomly while students find each letter you name and place it on the arc.
- Give a clue about a letter and have students name the letter you are thinking of. (For example, say, *I'm thinking of a letter that has one big line and three little lines and comes after* **D** *and before* **G**.)

Talking Points for Professional Development:
▸ Note the clarification of instructions into Spanish.
▸ What was the purpose/benefit of singing the vowels louder than the others?
▸ In Part 2 of the demonstration, students were relatively fast at mapping letters to sounds. Think of one change that might have helped reinforce prior teaching (e.g., making the vowels a different color).

Letter Naming

Familiarity with letters, gained by many opportunities to work with manipulative materials, and letter naming accuracy must precede any fluency drill. Drills must be very brief and game-like.

Lesson Component:

Letter knowledge.

Objective:

Students will fluently name all upper- and lowercase letters in random order.

Materials:

- Letter flash cards.
- Letter speed drills—randomly ordered uppercase, lowercase, or both.
- Uppercase and lowercase sets of plastic letters.

Instructional Procedure—Flash Card Drill:

- Shuffle uppercase, lowercase, or mixed-case letter flash card deck. Ask students to name as many letters as they can in one minute. Keep track of any incorrect responses and re-teach those letters.
- Have students practice the drill in pairs, taking turns being the "teacher."
- Time students while they place all plastic letters in order on the alphabet arc. Take one letter away while students hide their eyes, and see how quickly they can identify the missing letter.

Instructional Procedure—One-Minute Speed Drill:

- Pair students and have them name letters in random order. Each partner takes a turn being the teacher and checking the accuracy of the other partner's letter naming.

When proficiency is achieved, stop the practice!

Scaffolding Technique—*b/d* Confusion:

- Hold your hands in front of you, with your palms facing you. Form two fists, leaving your thumbs pointing up. Hold your fists together. Show students that this formation looks like a bed, with your left hand forming the shape of the letter *b* and your right hand forming the shape of the letter *d*. Students can check whether a letter is a *b* or *d* by holding the appropriate fist next to the print.

Talking Points for Professional Development:

▶ What other techniques do you know to help children discriminate between *b* and *d*?

▶ How can you ensure that students use their left hand to use the *b* recognition technique?

Letter Formation

If habits of directionality and spatial control are established early, handwriting will be more automatic and fluent and will be less effortful. Good letter formation facilitates spelling and composition in later grades. This lesson's demonstration shows the use of numbered arrows, verbal cues, and large motor practice of basic strokes.

Lesson Component:
Letter knowledge.

Objective:
Students will form letters within defined spaces using learned strokes.

Materials:
- Individual white boards with lines for letter formation.
- Dry-erase markers and pencils.
- Preprimer or primer writing paper with lines and spaces well defined.

Instructional Procedure—Forming Letters:

I DO
- Model the formation of the letter on the board. Either sit side-by-side with students or model with your back to them so that they can see your arm move. Label the lines and write within them (top, middle dotted, and baseline).
- Describe each stroke as you make it. Say, *To make the letter **b**, start at the top line and make a straight line down to the baseline. Make a curve up, forward, and around.*

WE DO
- Model while students practice. Trace the letter large in the air or on a carpet square. Trace dotted lines.

YOU DO
- Ask students to make several letters in a row and to select the best one. Have them practice on the white board and then on paper.

Scaffolding Techniques:
- Use wooden shapes to demonstrate and describe upper case and lower case letters (big lines, little lines, big curves, and little curves) such as those used in *Handwriting Without Tears* by Janice Z. Olsen (http://www.hwtears.com).
- Color code the top, middle, and bottom lines of writing paper for primary writing. Put an arrow or green margin on the left to signify left-right directionality.

Talking Points for Professional Development:

▶ Can the instruction "at the top" lead to confusion? Why? How would you change it?

▶ Skywriting is a great technique. When the teacher turns her back to model the activity, what does she miss?

▶ When students print a line of letters, they often get sloppy toward the end of the line. Might there be an advantage to having a student print each letter next to an example instead of having students write a line of letters, some of which may be sloppy?

▶ Note how the teacher can individualize not only her language instruction but the level of language.

Print-Related Vocabulary (Phase I)

If students are unfamiliar with the parts of books, how books are read, or the language used to describe the linguistic units (letter, word, sentence) or how they are ordered, explicit teaching will be necessary.

Lesson Component:

Concepts of print and vocabulary of instruction.

Objective:

Students will recognize and follow directions with terms *letter*, *word*, and *sentence*, as well as ordinal counting words *first, second, third*, and *last*.

Materials:

- Word cards.
- Plastic letters on a magnetic board.
- A simple sentence on a sentence strip, cut into individual words.
- Big book or book with large print for the group to follow.

Instructional Procedure—Letters, Words, and Sentences:

I DO

- Tell students they will learn the difference between a letter, a word, and a sentence.
- Put a word card out on the table. Say, *This is a written word.* Put another word on the table. Ask, *Is this a word?* (Yes.)
- Say, *Each word has some letters in it.* Put some individual plastic letters far apart on the magnetic board .
- Say, *Point to a letter.* (Students take turns pointing to individual letters.) Practice distinguishing words from letters with several more cards, calling on individual students.
- Put the whole sentence together and read it. Say, *This whole group of words is a sentence. Listen to how it sounds. What is the whole group of words?* (A sentence.) *This is the first word, the second word, and the third word; this is the last word.*

WE DO

- Say, *Let's play a game.* Make a word with plastic letters. Ask students to point to a letter, then have them point to a word. Put words into simple sentences. Ask students to use the labels *letter, word,* and *sentence* for these units of print as students identify them.

YOU DO

- Ask students to point to a word, letter, or sentence in the big book.
- In succeeding lessons, elaborate on the ordinal counting words (the beginning and ending, the first and last words, and so forth).

Talking Points for Professional Development:

▸ Why is teaching print-related vocabulary important?

▸ How does the teacher scaffold instruction?

▸ This segment introduces many concepts. If this were not a demonstration lesson, should more time be given to introducing each concept (letter, word, sentence, upper-and lowercase, punctuation)?

Print-Related Vocabulary (Phase II)

Lesson Component:
Concepts of print and vocabulary of instruction.

Objective:
Students will recognize and name the front, back, title, author, illustrations, and written words in books; will hold a book correctly; and will know that reading of text proceeds from left to right and top to bottom.

Materials:
Children's books with illustrations and standard "book parts."

Instructional Procedure—Book Features:

I DO
- Hold a book with the cover facing students. Say, *The front of this book has the title.* Point to the title and say, *This is the title. The title tells what the book is about.*

WE DO
- Say, *Point to the title with me. Is the title on the front or the back of the book?* (The front.) *Where is the title?* (On the front.) *What does the title tell us?* (It tells us what the book is about.)

YOU DO
- Give each student a book. Ask each student in turn to show the front of the book, point to the title, and say that the title tells us what the book is about.
- Use the same process for the illustrations, the back of the book, and the author's name.
- Play a find-it game about a new book, asking students the following questions:

    Where is the title? Point to it.

    Is this the front or the back of the book?

    Where should I start reading the words on this page?

    Where will I finish reading the words on this page?

Instructional Points for Professional Development:
- Why is teaching print-related vocabulary important?
- Why does the teacher continue to go through the whole sequence (e.g., first, second, and third)?
- How does she scaffold instruction? What else could she have done to help Alexis remember the sentence?
- What additional structure could be provided for a student who doesn't know ordinal counting words?

One-to-One Correspondence

Some students need to begin at the beginning, learning what *word* means. The video demonstration of this lesson shows how to use print itself to show children how words are spaced on the page. An alternative approach uses colored blocks to stand for separate words that can be added, taken away, or substituted in a sentence.

Lesson Component:
Concepts of print.

Objective:
Students will track words in sentences, pointing to each word as it is read aloud.

Materials:
- Simple sentences composed by you, beginning with one-syllable words only.
- Big book or sentence written on a sentence strip.

Instructional Procedure:

I DO
- Say a simple sentence, such as *"The cat ran up the tree."* Say the sentence again with a slight pause between words as you clap for each word in the sentence.

WE DO
- Have students repeat the sentence you say and clap as they say each word.

YOU DO
- Give students a sentence and have them repeat it while clapping for each word. Have them say and clap the words in several more simple sentences.

I DO
- Review the concept of a word by showing how each word in print in a big book or sentence strip is separated by a space.

WE DO
- Have students point to words in a sentence with you as you read and point to each word.

YOU DO
- Ask students to point to each word as you read a simple sentence.

Alternate Procedure: Using Colored Squares

Objective:

Students will identify, add, delete, and substitute tokens (squares) for words in sentences.

Materials:

- Six to eight different colored squares (felt or construction paper), one set per student.
- Teacher set of eight different colored felt squares, magnetized for use on magnetic board.
- Alternative: Use an overhead projector with transparent, colored acetate squares.
- Sentences to be composed by you (see the following examples).

Instructional Procedure:

I DO

- Say a sentence, such as *"The dog is sleeping."* Place four colored squares, left to right, on the magnet board. Repeat the sentence, pointing to each square as you say the word. (Words are not written. The words below are only to illustrate what you are saying.)

The	dog	is	sleeping.

- Touch each colored square as you say the words with students. (For variety, you can ask students to repeat the sentence in soft, loud, slow, or fast voices.)
- Say, *Each square stands for a word. What word is this?* (Point to squares in random order as children name the corresponding words.)

WE DO

- Practice with several more sentences.

  (I like to play baseball. Can we go to the zoo? My sister's name is Natasha.)

YOU DO

- Pass out a set of colored squares to each student. Say a new sentence. Ask students to place colored squares for each word, while you place your squares.
- Touch and say the sentence together
- Practice with three to six word sentences, such as the following:

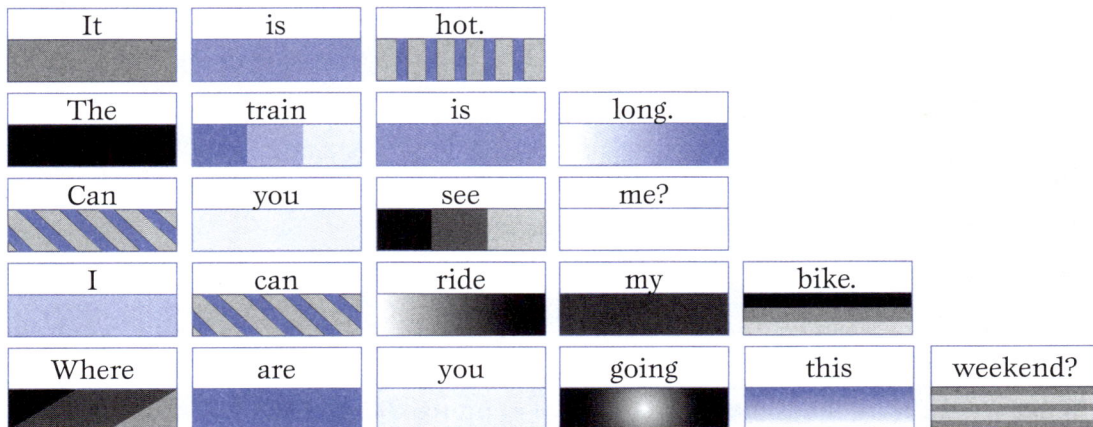

It	is	hot.			

The	train	is	long.		

Can	you	see	me?		

I	can	ride	my	bike.	

Where	are	you	going	this	weekend?

- Add words to sentences. Start with the sentence "The dog is sleeping." Add a word and demonstrate with a colored square. The sentence becomes "The *brown* dog is sleeping."

The	dog	is	sleeping.

The	brown	dog	is	sleeping.

- Substitute words in sentences. Start with the sentence, "The brown dog is sleeping." Change *sleeping* to *running* or *The* to *My*. (First and last words are easiest.) Model for students, then have them practice.

The	brown	dog	is	sleeping.

The	brown	dog	is	running.

My	brown	dog	is	running.

My	brown	cat	is	running.

My	white	cat	is	running.

My	white	cat	likes	running.

- Delete words in sentences: Start with the sentence, "My white cat likes running." Change the sentence to "My cat likes running." Model and practice with additional sentences.

My	white	cat	likes	running.

My	cat	likes	running.

Sentence examples:

"Here comes my big brother." "Here comes my brother."

"Where are you going tomorrow?" "Where are you going?"

"The brown chair is by the table." "The chair is by the table."

Talking Points for Professional Development:

▸ Note the use of "I do, We do, You do."

▸ Note how the teacher ensures success for each student by having each point when she feels relatively certain they will be successful.

▸ What are the techniques the teacher uses to reinforce the students?

▸ Note how the teacher only focuses on other technical words incidentally; she gives a quick definition and moves on (e.g., capital letter, uppercase letter).

Does It Make Sense?

Using direct teaching and practice, you can establish for children, even before they read, that what is read should make sense.

Lesson Component:
Concepts of print and vocabulary of instruction.

Objective:
Students will learn to expect that words they read will make sense.

Materials:
Sentences created by you, some that make sense and some that don't.

Instructional Procedure:

I DO
- Tell students that when they read or are read to, the words should make sense. For example, the words *We ran away as fast as we could* make sense, but *We fast away ran could* do not.

WE DO
- Say some more sentences, encouraging students to agree on which ones make sense and which ones don't.

YOU DO
- Call on individual students to tell you whether a sentence makes sense or not.

Talking Points for Professional Development:

▶ Note how the teacher concludes the lesson with restatement of the purpose. Would it help to both start and finish the lesson with the question "why?"

▶ Note how the teacher frequently asks students to say what she's saying. Why is that an important instructional tool?

▶ Note how the teacher handles the extra input from the boy. Was her technique effective in managing his behavior, honoring his communication, and staying on task?

▶ How could colored squares be used to facilitate instruction of this concept?

Part 2: Teaching Phoneme Awareness

What is the difference between phonological awareness discussed in Part 1 and phonemic awareness presented here?

Phonological awareness encompasses phoneme awareness, but also includes understanding how to identify and manipulate words, syllables, and onset and rime. Phoneme awareness is the most difficult level of phonological awareness. Students who have difficulty with phoneme awareness tasks often need phonological awareness instruction as described in Part 1.

For whom is phoneme awareness instruction important?

Students who benefit from direct teaching of phoneme awareness are those who are not yet able to orally segment or blend the single speech sounds in one-syllable words with accuracy and fluency. These students exhibit one or more of the following:

- They are typically below benchmark on DIBELS Phoneme Segmentation Fluency (PSF).
- They may be unable to identify first and last sounds in words.
- They may not know how to discriminate similar sounds in English (e.g., /sh/ and /ch/, or /w/ and /r/).
- They may be unable to identify vowel sounds in words.
- They usually guess at written words on the basis of one or two of the sounds the letters represent, instead of blending all the sounds together.
- heir spelling may include only one or two of the sounds in the word.

Do older students ever need phoneme awareness instruction?

About 90 % of older poor readers show weaknesses in reading skills that depend on phoneme awareness. These weaknesses manifest themselves in a number of ways, including:

- An inability to sound out unfamiliar words even though the student knows the letter sounds. (A student who knows letter sounds yet cannot read the word correctly is having difficulty blending phonemes into words.)

- Poor spelling. If a student can't segment the sounds in a word or has trouble breaking a word into syllables, spelling is likely to be very poor.
- Students mispronounce or confuse similar sounding words, such as *Pacific* and *specific*. Additional work on the perception and recall of syllables and speech sounds may be helpful to these students.

Why is phoneme awareness important?

English uses an alphabetic writing system in which the letters, singly and in combination, represent single speech sounds. People who can identify phonemes in orally spoken words or blend spoken phonemes into words have the foundation skill for using the alphabetic code. Without phoneme awareness, students may be mystified by the print system and how it relates to the spoken word.

Phoneme segmentation and blending abilities are correlated with beginning reading. Even before students learn to read, we can predict with a good deal of accuracy how children will do in reading if we can measure their knowledge of letter sounds and names and the breadth of their vocabulary.

A number of research studies have shown that instruction in speech sound awareness reduces and alleviates reading and spelling difficulties. Teaching speech sounds explicitly and directly also accelerates children's learning of the alphabetic code. Therefore, classroom instruction for beginning readers should include phoneme awareness activities. For students who exhibit phoneme awareness weaknesses, such as difficulty producing rhyming words or difficulty segmenting and blending phonemes in words, we can take preventive action and teach them the foundation skills they need to know.

How should we teach phoneme awareness?

1. Follow a progression of task difficulty, moving from the easiest tasks to the most difficult:
   - Identify and match the initial sounds in words, then final and middle sounds (e.g., "Which picture begins with /m/?").
   - Segment and produce an initial sound, then final and middle sounds (e.g., "What sound does *zoo* start with?").
   - Blend sounds into words (e.g., "Listen: /f/ /ee/ /t/. Say it fast.").
   - Segment the phonemes in two or three sound words, moving to four and five sounds as the student becomes proficient (e.g., "The word is *eyes*. Stretch and say the sounds. /ī/ /z/").
   - Manipulate phonemes by removing, adding, or substituting sounds (e.g., "smoke without the /m/.") (Chain the sounds in words *lamp, camp, cramp, crimp,* and *crimps* with colored blocks.)
2. Focus the student's attention on *sound* before you introduce letters. Tasks should be auditory and verbal prior to the focus on letters. Continue with phoneme awareness tasks until you are sure the student has his or her "auditory antennae" directed toward speech.
3. Encourage *mouth* awareness. Phonemes are speech gestures as well as speech sounds. Correct articulation of the sounds is very important in developing awareness of them. Ask students whether their mouths are open or closed when they make the sound. Ask them if they are using their tongue, teeth, or lips when they make the sound.

4. Include all phonemes in the instruction. All phonemes can be taught, including all vowel sounds (such as /ŏŏ/ in *foot*) and phonemes represented by digraphs (such as /ch/ in *itch* or /th/ in *that*).*

5. Involve the hand, eye, body, and mouth whenever possible. Gestures, pictures, and key words represented by objects are all valuable tools.

6. A few brief activities, requiring about 10–15 minutes per day, are all that most young children need to improve awareness of speech.

* *Understanding of speech sound production is essential.* Language Essentials for Teachers of Reading and Spelling (LETRS) Module 2 *provides detailed information on the features of sound production. The LETRS Interactive CD-ROM is another valuable tool for learning the complete consonant and vowel inventories of English.*

DVD Navigation

Part 2: Teaching Phoneme Awareness			
For students who are below benchmark on DIBELS PSF.			
Demonstration Video	Activity Name	Page	Time (minutes)
	Introduction to Part 2		22:06
Single Phonemes			
1	Speech Sounds With Gestures	32	11:37
2	Tracking Single Phonemes	34	12:56
3	Beginning Phonemes Professional Development Session	36	8:34 6:16
Segmentation and Blending			
4	Ending Phonemes	40	6:55
5	Blending Phonemes	43	4:36
6	Segmenting Phonemes Professional Development Session	46	4:03 5:41
7	Sound Chains	49	4:37
8	Sound Boxes With Print Professional Development Session	51	7:51 9:07

Speech Sounds With Gestures

Students learn the identity of speech sounds by pairing them with gestures. Gestures then help students say phonemes with emphasis and clarity and help them recall sounds on cue.

Lesson Component:
Phoneme identification.

Objective:
Students will articulate separate speech sounds with the help of a key word or gesture.

Materials:
List of gestures and key words for each speech sound (see Appendix E).

Instructional Procedure:

I DO
- Tell students you will practice saying separate phonemes or sounds.
- Model the articulation of a target phoneme (/ch/).
- Say /ch/ is the first sound in chin, and demonstrate the gesture (point to chin).

WE DO
- Say the phoneme and make the gesture with students.

YOU DO
- Each student gets a turn to say the phoneme and make the gesture, or to make the gesture for others to say the phoneme.
- Students practice associating a few phonemes and gestures at a time, gradually accumulating associations for most phonemes.

Extension Games:

- **Relay game.** Students line up in two lines. When you make a gesture, the student at the beginning of a team's line makes the sound. If the student misses, the student first in the other team's line gets a chance. Every correct response gets a point. The Relay game can be played with key objects or pictures in a bag or box where the leader of the line reaches in, picks a picture or object, and gives the sound.

- **Thumbs up.** Pick a target sound, such as /r/. When you say a word, phrase, or sentence (slowly paced to give response time), students hold thumbs up every time they hear the sound.

- **Musical sounds.** Students sit in a circle. Music plays while students pass sound cards or objects around the circle. When the music stops, students are called on to say the name of the object and the sound it represents.

Note: These games should be brief (1–5 minutes) and fun reinforcement activities.

Talking Points for Professional Development:

▶ Why does the teacher start out with /s/? What are the advantages, disadvantages?

▶ Why might a gesture be better than a picture for helping students remember sounds?

▶ Note the use of higher-level language (e.g., *continuants*). Is it OK to use this language with students of this age?

Tracking Single Phonemes

Before students are asked to isolate sounds from spoken words, practice tracking single sounds that are the same or different, using colored tiles to represent the sounds.

Lesson Component:
Phoneme identification, counting, and comparison.

Objective:
Students will represent a sequence of two to three phonemes with colored tiles, showing which ones are the same or different.

Materials:
- Colored tiles (five for each student, at least two the same color).
- Teacher-prepared phoneme sequences list.

Instructional Procedure—Two-Phoneme Sequences:

I DO
- Ask students to show two tiles that are the same color and two that are a different color.
- Explain that one colored tile can show one phoneme, such as /t/.
- Say, *If I say two phonemes that are the same, such as /t/ /t/, we can use two tiles of the same color to show the phonemes.* (Touch and say.)
- Say, *If I say /t/ /s/, the phonemes are different, so I use two different colored tiles to show the phonemes.* (Touch and say.)

WE DO
- Say, *Listen: /m/ /m/. Now you say the phonemes /m/ /m/. They are the same, so we can use two tiles the same color to show the phonemes. Do it with me, and then touch and say with me.*
- *Now let's do /m/ /k/. Say the phonemes /m/ /k/. Are they the same or different? Show me with your tiles.* (Touch and say.)

YOU DO

- Each student gets a turn to listen, repeat, put the correct tiles out, and do touch and say.
Examples of two-phoneme sequences:

/v/ /d/

/ă/ /ō/

/d/ /d/

/g/ /sh/

/b/ /d/

/ī/ /ou/

/ch/ /ch/

/th/ /th/

Instructional Procedure—Three-Phoneme Sequences:

WE DO

- Say, *Now let's do three phonemes. If two are the same, use the same color tiles.*
  Let's do /a/ /d/ /d/ together.
- *Your turn to do three phonemes.*
Examples of three-phoneme sequences:

/s/ /k/ /ī/

/ĕ/ /d/ /f/

/ch/ /g/ /ŭ/

/ĭ/ /ĭ/ /z/

/v/ /ă/ /v/

/w/ /w/ /y/

/sh/ /sh/ /z/

/ch/ /j/ /ch/

/ŏ/ /ŏ/ /ŭ/

Talking Points for Professional Development:

▸ What are the steps used to scaffold this instruction?

▸ How might this activity support building phoneme memory for students with poor memory?

▸ Note that when the teacher does /m/ /m/, his pitch is different (rising on the first and falling on the second). Could students say that the sounds are different when this happens?

Beginning Phonemes

Several activities are demonstrated that give students practice recognizing, matching, and then isolating a beginning speech sound. All sounds are fair game in these activities, as spelling is not involved.

Step 1: Matching Phonemes

Lesson Component:
Phoneme identification and isolation.

Objective:
Students will recognize, match, and pronounce the first phoneme in a spoken word.

Materials:
- Colored tiles.
- Piece of paper with three adjacent boxes on it. Boxes should be slightly larger than colored tiles. (These are called Elkonin boxes.)
- Word lists.
- Picture cards.

Instructional Procedure:

- Introduce the goal. Say, *We will be listening for the first sound in each word.*
- *The phoneme of the day is /m/.*
- *Say it with me, /m/.*
- *The word mop begins with the phoneme /m/, mop.*
- *The words mouse, miss, and map all begin with the phoneme /m/, too.*
- *The word dog begins with a different phoneme.*

I DO
- *When I hear the phoneme /m/ at the beginning of a word, I will put a colored tile in the first box. Remember, we always go from left to right to show where the phoneme is in the word.*
- *If the phoneme at the beginning of the word is not /m/, I leave my first box blank and give a thumbs down.*
- *When I say the word mug, I hear the phoneme /m/ at the beginning, so I move a tile into the box.*
- *When I say the word boat, I don't hear the phoneme /m/ at the beginning, so I put thumbs down, and I don't put a tile in the first box.*

WE DO

- Say, *Let's do one together.*
- *If I say the word* **move,** *do you hear the phoneme /**m**/ at the beginning?* (Yes).
- *Put a tile in the first box to show /**m**/ is at the beginning of the word.*
- *Let's try another word:* **sing.**
- *I don't hear the phoneme /**m**/ at the beginning, do you? So, we don't put a tile in the first box and we put thumbs down.*

YOU DO

- Give each student a turn to listen, repeat the sound and the word, decide if there is a match, and then move a tile in the first box if there is a match.

Words for identifying /m/ in the beginning of a target word:

mad

mark

shop (no)

mud

talk (no)

mess

net (no)

moan

name (no)

more

Words for identifying /s/ in the beginning of a target word:

cent

sale

boss (no)

seen

kiss (no)

self

sick

zip (no)

shine (no)

soon

zoo (no)

Step 2: Sorting Pictures

Objective:
Students will match two pictured objects that begin with the same sound.

Materials:
Picture cards with examples of words beginning with two or three different target sounds.

Instructional Procedure:
- Introduce the task. Explain that students will match the beginning sound of each picture to the beginning sounds of the picture on the header cards you put out on the table.
- Distribute picture cards in the deck, such as cards with objects beginning with /m/ and /s/.
- Lead one or two match-ups. Ask students to say the name of the picture they have, and say the sound the picture begins with.
- Rotate turns in the group. Ask other students to check the student whose turn it is.

Step 3: Isolating and Articulating Beginning Phonemes

Objective:
Students will isolate and articulate initial phonemes.

Materials:
- Word lists.
- Picture cards.

Instructional Procedure:
- Select sets of cards with two target phonemes, such as /m/ and /s/.
- Review the articulation of each sound and its corresponding gesture.
- Ask students to draw a picture card from the deck.
- The student (or teacher) names the card. The student repeats the name if it is unfamiliar.
- Ask the student to say the beginning phoneme while making the phoneme gesture.

38

Part 2 • *Teaching Reading Essentials*

Alternative Activity: Beginning Phonemes—Odd One Out Game

Materials:
Three to five sets of picture cards that begin with the same sound.

Instructional Procedure:
- Place four picture cards on the table, three with the same beginning sound.
- Ask students to say the names of each picture (if students have not seen these pictures before, it is best for the teacher to name them first to avoid confusion) and find the one that does not begin with same sound. Model saying each word slowly and carefully, exaggerating the beginning sound.
- Ask students to say the beginning sound of the pictures that begin with the same sound, and say the beginning sound of the picture that begins differently. Refer to gesture, picture, or object cues as necessary.
- **Picture pick-up.** Change the game by passing out to each student sets of two to three pictures that begin with different sounds. Students put the pictures face up in front of them. Say a sound. If the student has a picture that begins with that sound, he or she should pick it up and hold it. The object of the game is to have all pictures picked up.

Talking Points for Professional Development:

▸ How does the teacher incorporate multisensory experience with this activity? How many senses are tapped?

▸ How could this activity be combined with vocabulary building? Should the cards be selected to *only* represent those words in students' oral language vocabularies? (For example, the words *medal* and *seahorse* might not be in students' vocabularies, especially if some students are ELL.)

▸ If you decide to incorporate these words into a vocabulary lesson, how will you ensure that you keep the focus on beginning phonemes?

▸ Why is it important to make sure that all students can identify initial phonemes easily and quickly?

▸ Why concentrate on only one or two phonemes at a time?

▸ Could these activities be conducted with more than two or three phonemes?

▸ Each of these activities could also be used with ending phonemes.

Ending Phonemes

Ending phonemes are more challenging for students to hear or be aware of because those sounds may not be articulated with the same emphasis or clarity as beginning sounds. One important job of the teacher is to exaggerate the articulation of ending phonemes during these exercises.

Lesson Component:
Phoneme awareness.

Objective:
Students will recognize and pronounce the last phoneme in a spoken word.

Step 1: Using Colored Squares and Sound Boxes

Materials:
- Colored felt squares with magnets on the back for the teacher.
- White board.
- Colored tiles for students.
- Piece of paper with three sound boxes on it (Elkonin boxes).

Instructional Procedure:

- Introduce listening for and matching phonemes at the end of words.
- Say, *The phoneme of the day is /**sh**/.*
- Say */sh/.*
- Say, *The word **wish** ends with the phoneme /**sh**/: wish, /sh/.*
- *The words **lash**, **rush**, and **mash** all end with the phoneme /**sh**/, too.*
- *The word **tip** ends with a different phoneme.*
- *When I hear the phoneme of the day at the end of a word, I can put a colored tile in the last box. Remember, we always go from left to right to show that the phoneme matches.*
- *If the phoneme at the end of the word doesn't match, I leave my box blank and put my thumbs down.*
- *When I say the word **rash**, I hear the phoneme /**sh**/ at the end, so I move a tile into the last box.*
- *When I say the word **rack**, I don't hear the phoneme /**sh**/ at the end, so I don't put a tile in the last box and I put my thumbs down.*

(I DO)

WE DO
- Say, *Let's do one together:* **fish**. *Does the word end with /**sh**/?* (Yes.) *What should we do?* (Put a tile in the last box.)
- *Let's try another:* **sit**.
- *I don't hear the phoneme /**sh**/ at the end, do you? So, we don't put a tile in the last box. We put thumbs down.*

YOU DO
- Each student gets a turn to listen, repeat the sound and the word, and decide if the target phoneme is the last sound of the word.

Step 2: Using Pictures

Materials:
- Sets of pictures, one set with and two sets without a target phoneme in the final position.
- List of three-word sets, one word with and two words without the target sound.

Instructional Procedure:

I DO
- Introduce a target sound.
- Review the articulation and gesture for the target sound.
- Show students a set of three pictures, and have them repeat the names of pictures as you point to each.
- Explain that one picture ends with the target sound and the others do not.
- Show students which word ends with the target sound.

WE DO
- Display three pictures and name them with students.
- Help students identify which picture ends with the target sound. For example, say, *Which picture ends with /**t**/?*

YOU DO
- Practice this procedure with several of the target sounds for the day.
- Ask students to identify the picture with the ending target sound.

Next Steps

- Say a word and ask students to say the sound and make the gesture for the last sound in the word. Say, *If I say **Tom**, you will say /**m**/ and show me the gesture that represents /**m**/. . .* (Rubbing the tummy.)

- Say a word and ask students if the target sound is in the beginning of the word or at the end of the word. For example, say, *This time I will give you a word, and you will tell me where our target sound is. The word is **mail**. Where is the /**m**/—at the beginning or the end of the word?*

- Use sound boxes, and have students move a marker into the first or last sound box to show the position of the target phoneme in a spoken word.

Talking Points for Professional Development:

▸ Why is the teacher able to speed up the pace?

▸ What happens when the pace changes?

▸ Is there an advantage to using *only* two boxes? Is there a disadvantage?

▸ Should the teacher distinguish between the letter *o* and /ŏ/ when he's asking for location? Why? Why not?

Blending Phonemes

Sound blending begins with two- and three-sound words, preferably words that begin with continuant sounds that are easy to stretch out during blending. "Touch and Say" is a routine established here. Students say each sound as you point to the block representing it, then they blend the sounds together as you sweep your finger from left to right under the blocks.

Lesson Component:

Phoneme awareness.

Objective:

Students will blend two to three phonemes into a whole word.

Materials:

- Words with two to three phonemes for sound blending.
- Colored, magnetized felt squares for the teacher.
- Colored squares on sound blending cards for students.
- Key word picture cards.

Instructional Procedure—Two-Phoneme Words:

I DO
- Say, *I'm going to say some sounds slowly, and you'll help me put them together to make a word.*
- Put two squares on board a few inches apart while you say, *Listen. /s/ /ē/.*
- Push the squares together and say, *Say it fast.* (See.)

WE DO
- Put out two squares that are not touching, and say, *Now you do it.*
- *Touch your squares while you say the sounds with me, /s/ /ē/.*
- *Now, push the squares together and say the word fast.* (See.)
- Try a few more words with two sounds: /t/ /ō/, toe; /ā/ /k/, ache; /z/ /o͞o/, zoo. Say the sounds, then blend the word. Have students touch their squares and say the sounds while you model on the board. They can sweep their finger left to right while they "say the sounds fast."

- Each student gets a turn to repeat phonemes, using tiles to touch and say and blend the word.

Examples of two-phoneme words:

> /g/ /ō/ (go)
>
> /ā/ /p/ (ape)
>
> /ē/ /ch/ (each)
>
> /ĭ/ /n/ (in)
>
> /ī/ /s/ (ice)
>
> /y/ /o͞o/ (you)
>
> /sh/ /ī/ (shy)
>
> /ar/ /t/ (art)
>
> /ou/ /t/ (out)
>
> /b/ /oi/ (boy)

Instructional Procedure—Three-Phoneme Words:

- Introduce blending three phonemes to make words.
- Demonstrate using tiles, three-sound boxes, and touch and say to blend three phonemes to make a word (e.g., /m/ /ă/ /t/, mat).

- Using the phonemes / /s/ /ō/ /k/ (soak), say, *Let's do one together*.

- Each student gets a turn to repeat phonemes, using tiles to touch and say and blend the word.
- Select three students to stand side-by-side. Give each student a key word card for a sound. Have students say their sounds in order, blending the sounds into a whole word.

Examples of three-phoneme words:

> /k/ /ē/ /p/ (keep)
>
> /g/ /ā/ /m/ (game)
>
> /ch/ /ĭ/ /p/ (chip)
>
> /sh/ /ou/ /t/ (shout)
>
> /b/ /ă/ /g/ (bag)
>
> /k/ /oi/ /n/ (coin)
>
> /y/ /ĕ/ /l/ (yell)
>
> /s/ /ī/ /t/ (sight)
>
> /t/ /er/ /n/ (turn)
>
> /r/ /ē/ /ch/ (reach)

Talking Points for Professional Development:

▶ Has the teacher's instructional language changed since the early lessons?

▶ What prompts are given to produce the correct sounds?

▶ Why do students need to be able to blend sounds without letters?

▶ Why might this activity be especially important for students who come to kindergarten or first grade with large banks of sight words?

Segmenting Phonemes

Blending is usually easier for students than taking the sounds of a word apart. However, some students find segmenting easier than blending sounds. Segmentation is much easier when students are already familiar with the individual speech sounds of their language and can associate a gesture or key word with most of the sounds.

Lesson Component:
Phoneme awareness.

Objective:
Students will segment two and three phonemes in a whole word.

Materials:
- Words with two and three phonemes for sound segmentation.
- Colored, magnetized felt squares for the teacher.
- Colored blocks or chips, set of three of different colors (e.g., three red, three blue, three yellow) for each student.
- Sound box cards with two boxes and three boxes (Elkonin boxes).

Instructional Procedure—Two Sounds:

I DO
- Say, *I can break any word into its sounds. Listen.* **At. /ă/ /t/.** Put two squares on the board in sound boxes while you say, */ă/ /t/. What's the word?* (At.)

WE DO
- *Let's do some together. We'll say the word, then move the blocks into the boxes.* Have students say the word, and pull down a block into the two-square grid as they say each sound slowly.
- Allow more practice with words that have two sounds, such as /t/ /ō/, toe; /ā/ /k/, ache; /z/ /o͞o/, zoo; and add /ā/ /d/, demonstrating as students follow you.

YOU DO
- Say a word, then ask students to segment the sounds with colored tiles in the Elkonin sound boxes. Have students "say it and move it" with their blocks. Finally, have students sweep their finger left to right under the sounds while they "say the sounds fast."
- More two-sound words are: *so, pay, me, up, my, may, see, say, do, go, we, us, be, ice, to, show, ash.*

Instructional Procedure—Three Sounds:

I DO
- Say, *I can break any word into its sounds. We'll use sound boxes to show the sounds. Listen.* **Mat**. */m/ /ă/ /t/.*
- Put three squares on the board in sound boxes while you say, */m/ /ă/ /t. What's the word?* (Mat.)

WE DO
- Say, *Now you try it. When I say, "Say it and move it," you move a block into each box as you say the sound.*
- Ask students to say the word, then pull down a block into a square on the grid as they say each sound slowly.
- Finish by saying the whole word again, sweeping your fingers from left to right under the sounds.

YOU DO
- Use pictures of words with three sounds for pairs of students to practice pulling blocks or chips into the boxes as they say the sounds.

Alternate Procedure—Finger Stretching:

- Explain that students will use their fingers to identify the sounds in words.
- Demonstrate the following steps to students:
    1. Hold a fist out in front of your body.
    2. Say a word with three sounds, such as *moon*.
    3. Beginning with the thumb, put up one digit as you say each sound in the word. For example, with the word *moon*, the thumb would represent /m/, the forefinger would represent /o͞o/, and the middle finger would represent /n/.
    4. Blend the sounds together as you close your fist, pulling it toward your body. For students who struggle with left-to-right orientation, it can be helpful to provide reinforcement by moving the arm across the body when pulling together the sounds.

Alternate Procedure—Head, Waist, Toes:

I DO
- Say, *Watch me. I can take a three-sound word apart and touch one sound on my head, one sound on my waist, and one sound on my toes.*
- *Let's do* **dish**. */d/ /i/ /sh/. Which sound is on my head? My waist? My toes?*

WE DO
- Say, *Let's do some together.*
- Use words such as *dish, reach, can, soup, loud,* and *pitch*.

YOU DO
- Each student gets a turn to repeat a word and segment using the head, waist, and toes technique.
- Ask questions, such as *"Where is (phoneme)?"* and *"What is the middle phoneme?"*

Scaffolding:

- Show students how many sounds there are by using the right number of sound boxes. The point of this exercise is the oral production of sounds in a one-syllable word. Go back to earlier lessons if three sounds are too difficult.

- Progress to words with four and five sounds very gradually as students become able to segment the sounds in consonant blends.

Talking Points for Professional Development:

▶ How important is modeling before you ask students to respond?

▶ Many teachers say that head, waist, toes helps their students who have difficulty hearing middle sounds. Why might this activity be better than finger stretching or colored blocks for some students as they learn to segment sounds?

▶ Why do you think segmenting sounds is good predictor of how well students will learn to read?

Sound Chains

Lesson Component:
Phoneme awareness.

Objective:
Students will substitute one phoneme for another to make a new word.

Materials:
- Words with three to four phonemes, differing by one sound only.
- Colored magnetized felt squares for the teacher.
- Colored blocks or chips (set of four of different colors, two of each color, for each student).

Instructional Procedure:

I DO
- Say, *Today we're going to listen for sounds that change in a word.*
- Put three squares of different colors on the board as you say, **night**. Touch and say, */n/ /ī/ /t/*. **Night**.
- Say, *I'm going to change something. This is* **night**. *Let's change it to* **light**. (Change the colored square for /n/.)
- *What did I change? That's right. I changed the first sound. I changed /n/ to /l/ to change* **night** *to* **light**.

WE DO
- Say, *Let's do some together. Listen for the sound that changes. Show me* **mess**. *Now change* **mess** *to* **guess**. Students say the word, put out three blocks, and then find which sound changed and change that color block.
- Students say the word they started with, what it changed to, and what sound changed.

YOU DO
- Give more practice, moving gradually to substitution of the last sound and then the middle sound.

  Note: This is not a spelling activity. Since sounds are the only thing of interest, words that differ only in one speech sound do not have to be spelled the same way. Words with digraph spellings can be used because digraphs represent one sound. Words with three sounds that can be used are:

Beginning Change	Ending Change	Middle Change
knees, peas	dock, doll	tip, top
boat, note	room, rude	miss, mess
much, such	bath, bash	hope, hype

Talking Points for Professional Development:

▸ When working on this activity, the teacher could be specific about what the student is doing right. One example would be to compliment the student on sounding out each word to "hear and feel" where the sound changed. Are there other examples?

▸ What skills need to be in place before the student is ready for sound chains?

▸ Why is it important for students to think about using a different color when sounds are different?

Sound Boxes With Print

As students learn to segment separate speech sounds in simple words and syllables, they can start to use letters to mark the sounds they identify. This activity provides the transition from speech sound analysis to spelling and teaches the alphabetic principle.

Lesson Component:
Phoneme awareness and phonics.

Objective:
Students will segment the sounds in simple words and spell them in Elkonin boxes that stand for each speech sound in the word.

Materials:
- Magnetic plastic letters.
- White boards and markers.
- Template for correct number of sound boxes (i.e., two, three, and four).
- List of words with letter-sound correspondences students know.

Instructional Procedure:

I DO
- Draw or put sound boxes on a white board. Select and place the letters needed to spell a word above the sound boxes.
- Say, *You already know how to move markers into sound boxes as you say the sounds in a word. Today I'll show you how to use letters for each sound.*
- Using a word like *fan,* say the word and then say the sounds, pulling the correct letter into each box as you say the sound.
- Touch and say by touching each letter and saying its sound; then, run your finger underneath the letters left to right and read the word.

WE DO
- Pass out the white boards and magnetic letter sets to each student.
- Say the word and have students repeat the word.
- With students, segment the sounds while pointing to boxes.
- With students, put letters into boxes while saying the sound.
- With students, touch and say.

YOU DO
- Give more practice and call on individual students.

Scaffolding:

- Start by giving students only the letters that will be used in the words they spell. As students become proficient, give them more letters so the choice of letters becomes more difficult.

- Give students Elkonin boxes with the exact number of sounds in each word. As students become more proficient, give them six Elkonin boxes so they have to decide how many sounds are in the word.

- Start with one letter for one sound in three-sound CVC words, then add digraphs, then blends.

- Use tiles that have digraphs and trigraphs on one tile to emphasize that one sound can equal more than one letter.

Talking Points for Professional Development:

▶ Why is this an important activity for beginning readers who have large banks of sight words?

▶ What makes the teacher's directions clear?

▶ How does the teacher give corrective feedback?

▶ What makes the word *frog* difficult and why?

▶ Why is the inside sound in the blend /st/ in *nest* not as difficult as the /r/ in *frog*?

Part 3: Teaching Beginning Reading and Writing

Who needs beginning reading and writing instruction?

Students who can benefit from the instruction modeled in this section are typically beginning or novice readers at the end of kindergarten or beginning of first grade. They are just learning phoneme-grapheme correspondences and are in what can be called the "partial alphabetic" stage of reading. They may also be remedial students of any age who have mastered the following skills:

- Know letter names.
- Can isolate beginning and ending speech sounds in words.
- Can orally blend two or three speech sounds together into a word.
- Know a few "sight" words in context.

These students may also exhibit the following weaknesses or deficits:

- Have difficulty reading unknown words because they do not utilize a phonics strategy for decoding words.
- Read "word by word" without phrasing.
- Are poor spellers, with only some letters accurately corresponding to sounds.

Students who can benefit from this instruction generally score below benchmark in DIBELS Nonsense Word Fluency (NWF) and/or Oral Reading Fluency (ORF), indicating a need for phonics instruction. However, they will score at or just below benchmark in Phoneme Segmentation Fluency (PSF) and Letter Naming Fluency (LNF), indicating they have some phoneme awareness and know their letter names.

Why is code-emphasis instruction necessary?

Some students learn the written code of English naturally and easily. They may learn to read just by being read to often, or they may learn phonics from just a few exposures to phonograms (word families), simple words, and so forth. Unfortunately, many students do not learn to read this easily.

Learning to read is neither easy nor natural for most students, especially those who show early signs of risk. (Early signs of risk include difficulty learning letter names or shapes, difficulty learning to rhyme, an inability to identify or isolate phonemes, and lack of response to good beginning reading instruction.) For many people, learning to read can be a protracted process, and success depends on the quality of teaching and the instructional program.

Understanding the basics of phonics (letter-sound correspondences) and development of rapid word recognition are tools students need to read texts on their own. Use of grapheme-phoneme (letter-sound) correspondences, familiar rime patterns, and meaningful word parts are all productive word-recognition strategies to use in beginning reading instruction. Students also need to learn the habit of checking their understanding of text to make sure the word they decoded or read makes sense.

Decodable text is used at early phases of reading instruction. It consists of sentences or stories in which a very high proportion of the words in the text have phonics patterns or sight words that have been taught explicitly. Decodable text is used with beginning readers so that they can practice applying what they have been taught about sound-symbol correspondences. As reading skill develops and students learn to accurately and fluently decode using phonics correspondences, leveled texts can be introduced for reading practice. Accuracy and independent word recognition are always emphasized before fluency in these lessons.

Many older poor readers need basic phonics instruction. They may have partial knowledge of phonics, in that they may use a few letters and the length of the word, coupled with context, as the basis for guessing at words as they read. These students may also misread small function words (e.g., *the* for *a*, *when* for *then*). Systematic teaching of phonics and an emphasis on accurate and fluent reading is the best treatment to help these older students develop a decoding strategy and become proficient readers.

Even those children who learn to read relatively easily benefit from a solid foundation in phonics and decoding. Phonics helps with spelling and helps students build accurate, independent word analysis skills that lead more quickly to reading fluency.

Several studies have shown that students who read well early tend to read more throughout their schooling. When we teach early reading using the most effective teaching methods virtually all children learn to decode well and accurately, establishing a foundation for being able to decode unfamiliar words as text becomes more difficult. Accurate decoding in combination with a good vocabulary insures that students have the basis for enjoying reading, as opposed to being frustrated because reading is too hard.

What are the components of a beginning reading lesson?

There are several steps in a beginning reading lesson. However, not all steps will be included in every lesson, and not every step will be included at all phases of teaching beginning reading. Programs vary in their relative emphasis on lesson components. Typical components are:

- State the lesson objective and purpose.
- Review what has been taught previously (sounds, phonics concepts, words, text).
- Identify sounds in spoken words (sound warm-up).
- Match letters to sounds (symbol-sound association) and sounds to letters (sound-symbol association).

- Teach the new sound-symbol correspondence pattern explicitly and directly.
- Blend sounds of newly taught letters together (touch and say) to make words
- Teach "heart words" (high-frequency words that do not follow phonics patterns taught) using visualization strategies.
- Practice building fluency with:
  Question and answer games
  Timed speed practice
  Pattern recognition
  Word sorting
- Read words in phrases and sentences, and ensure knowledge of word meanings during these activities.
- Use decodable passages for practicing reading and utilizing reading comprehension strategies.
- Spell words (word chains; dictation).
- Use writing that includes dictated sentences and supported, independent composition.

What content do we teach in a beginning code-emphasis program?

The content of instruction, or scope and sequence, should move from easier to more difficult print correspondences in a systematic progression. There is no one "right" progression, but the following are general guidelines that most programs follow:
- High-utility single consonants (*f, s, m, t, p*) and a short vowel (ă).
- All short vowels (wide contrasts such as /ă/ and /ĭ/ first).
- High-frequency "heart" words (irregularly spelled words that need to be learned "by heart"), three to five per week.
- All single consonants.
- Consonant oddities (*x, qu*).
- Consonant digraphs *(ch, sh, th, wh, -ck)*.
- Double final consonants (*f, l, s,* and *z*).
- Consonant blends, final and initial.
- Inflectional suffixes (*-s, -es, -ed,* and *-ing*).
- Hard and soft *c* and *g*.
- Trigraphs (*-tch, -dge*).
- Common rime patterns or "chunks" *(ink, ank, unk; all; ing)*.

How do we teach? What are the principles of instruction?

- Be *explicit*—explain *directly* what you want students to learn.
- Be *systematic*—teach parts within a map of the whole system.
- Use the principles of "I do, we do, you do" or "Model, lead, practice."
- Have students read aloud individually to demonstrate their knowledge of new concepts.
- Provide *cumulative* review.

- *Check for understanding* of each new concept taught; *reteach* if necessary.
- *Practice* for automaticity and fluency.
- *Apply* to reading phrases, sentences, and books.
- *Be clear about terms* and their meanings—letter, sound, syllable, word, meaningful part (morpheme), rime, phrase, sentence, and paragraph.
- Ask for *active* response and engagement; use hands, body, movable objects, vocal response (multisensory learning)
- Teach the most common, irregular sights words (heart words) a few at a time (three to five per week), with multisensory "tracing and saying" or visualization techniques.
- Link instruction to *meaning*. Always ask, Do students know what the words mean?
- Teach reading *comprehension* as soon as children can read connected text.

DVD Navigation

<table>
<tr><th colspan="4">Part 3: Teaching Beginning Reading and Writing</th></tr>
<tr><td colspan="4">For students who are below benchmark on DIBELS NWF and ORF.</td></tr>
<tr><th>Demonstration Video</th><th>Activity Name</th><th>Page</th><th>Time (minutes)</th></tr>
<tr><td></td><td>Introduction to Part 3</td><td></td><td>21:12</td></tr>
<tr><td colspan="4">Basic Routines</td></tr>
<tr><td>1</td><td>Heart Words</td><td>59</td><td>10:42</td></tr>
<tr><td>2</td><td>Short Vowel Sounds</td><td>61</td><td>9:38</td></tr>
<tr><td></td><td>Professional Development Session</td><td></td><td>12:24</td></tr>
<tr><td>3</td><td>Letter-Sound Correspondence</td><td>63</td><td>5:38</td></tr>
<tr><td>4</td><td>Spelling Chains</td><td>65</td><td>8:14</td></tr>
<tr><td colspan="4">A Complete Phonics Lesson on Short i Words</td></tr>
<tr><td>5</td><td>Phonemic Workout</td><td>67</td><td>3:12</td></tr>
<tr><td>6</td><td>Introducing New Letter Sounds</td><td>68</td><td>4:59</td></tr>
<tr><td>7</td><td>Building Real Words</td><td>70</td><td>8:03</td></tr>
<tr><td></td><td>Professional Development Session</td><td></td><td>8:34</td></tr>
<tr><td>8</td><td>Nonsense Words</td><td>72</td><td>5:22</td></tr>
<tr><td>9</td><td>The "Question and Answer" Game</td><td>73</td><td>5:08</td></tr>
<tr><td>10</td><td>Reading Word Patterns</td><td>74</td><td>4:03</td></tr>
<tr><td>11</td><td>Reading Nonsense Words</td><td>75</td><td>2:29</td></tr>
<tr><td>12</td><td>Fluency Builder</td><td>76</td><td>5:00</td></tr>
<tr><td>13</td><td>Reading Sentences</td><td>77</td><td>4:59</td></tr>
<tr><td></td><td>Professional Development Session</td><td></td><td>6:13</td></tr>
<tr><td>14</td><td>Dictation</td><td>79</td><td>9:11</td></tr>
<tr><td>15</td><td>Reading Decodable Books</td><td>81</td><td>2:24</td></tr>
<tr><td colspan="4">Teaching Spelling Patterns</td></tr>
<tr><td>16</td><td>Word Sorting With -ck</td><td>83</td><td>8:05</td></tr>
<tr><td></td><td>Professional Development Session</td><td></td><td>9:01</td></tr>
<tr><td>17</td><td>Consonant Blends</td><td>85</td><td>7:34</td></tr>
</table>

Fluency and Comprehension—Decodable Text			
18	Alternate Oral Reading	87	14:33
19	Choral Reading	89	12:07
	Professional Development Session		5:08
20	Word Recognition Strategy	91	15:34
	Professional Development Session		17:51
Fluency and Comprehension—Leveled Text			
21	Phrasing	93	9:38
22	Partner Reading	95	16:34
	Professional Development Session		10:02
23	Fluency Practice	97	7:52
Supported Writing			
24	Supported Group Writing	99	14:19
	Professional Development Session		12:45
25	Supported Independent Writing	100	17:32
Comprehensive, Integrated Lesson			
26	Comprehensive Lesson: Reading Decodable Text	101	34:10
	Professional Development Session		19:48

Heart Words

Heart words are those that do not follow regular, teachable phonic patterns. (We call them "heart" words because students have to learn irregular parts of the word "by heart.") The method for heart word instruction differs from phonics, in that students are encouraged to use visualization strategies and multisensory tracing, saying, and writing strategies to remember the words.

Lesson Component:
Automatic reading of high-frequency, irregular words.

Objective:
Students will read irregular words (heart words) as wholes, about one per second.

Materials:
- Magnetic teacher letter tiles, with heart tile.
- White boards and markers for students.
- Index cards.
- List of high-frequency, irregular words, to be introduced at the rate of two to five per week.

Instructional Procedure:
- Present two to three new irregular words (heart words) on flash cards, such as *said, they, was*. Explain that we call these words "heart" words because some parts that aren't spelled as we expect have to be learned "by heart."
- Spell an irregular word (*said*) with letter tiles. Ask students to identify the parts that are spelled the way we expect. (The *s* and *d* in *said*.)
- Ask students to identify the part that must be learned "by heart" and underline it. (The *ai* in *said*.) Use a heart tile or draw a heart above those letters to draw attention to that part of the word.
- Have students look at the word, say the word, and write the word with their finger in the air or on a rough board, rug, or salt tray as they spell it aloud. Have students repeat the word. When they are ready, students should cover the card and write the word from memory on the white board. Have students hold the white board up for you to check when they finish.
- Visualization can be practiced in the following way:
  - Teacher spells a word with letter tiles—(one letter tile for each letter).
  - Students take a mental picture of a word.
  - Teacher turns over the letter tiles.

- Students name the letters in random order, in backward order, and finally in correct sequence.

- Students write the word on their boards.

- Teacher turns letters so spelling shows and students check their answers.

- (Part of this visualization activity can consist of asking "What letter comes before the *a*?" "What letter comes after the *s*?")

• Students write the heart word on an index card. On the back of the card, they make a simple chart on which they will keep track of the number of times they have read or spelled the word correctly. If they can read and spell the word correctly three days in a row, they "own" the word and can bank it in their alphabetized word box.

Talking Points for Professional Development:

▶ What are the steps in the heart word technique?

▶ Note how the teacher emphasizes that we don't end with spelling backward. Why?

▶ What is the purpose of the camera?

▶ Notice that this method makes irregularly spelled words less overwhelming because students must memorize only parts of words, as opposed to being told that "these words just have to be memorized."

▶ Why might these visualization exercises be especially useful for students with orthographic weaknesses?

▶ How does the teacher respond when the student gives the name of the letter instead of the sound? Does this help?

▶ When the students said that the spelling for the middle sound in *said* is usually *a*, what sounds are they confusing? What could the teacher do to help students overcome that confusion?

Short Vowel Sounds

Students rehearse the short vowel sounds for letters by pairing them with gestures and stretching out the articulation of each sound.

Lesson Component:

Accurate, fast association of letters *a, e, i, o,* and *u* with short vowel sounds.

Objective:

Students will say the sound that the vowel letter represents, using a gesture based on a key word.

Materials:

- List of suggested guide words and gestures (see the appendix). (Alternatively, a list of pictures or objects to serve as guide words or key words.)
- Magnetic teacher letter tiles *a, e, i, o, u.*
- Apples, one for the teacher and one for each student.
- Student letter tiles, *a, e, i, o, u,* and white boards.
- Practice pages for producing short vowel sounds.

Instructional Procedure:

I DO
- State objective: To teach movements and guide words for each short vowel letter sound.
- Teach the vowel sound for each letter, giving motion and guide word; model "stretching out" the sound until the gesture is completed.

WE DO
- Practice making the motion and saying the sound while students point to the letter (Receptive practice). Practice pointing to the letter while students make the motion and say the sound (Expressive practice).
- Rehearse the difference between short *e* and short *i*, pointing out the difference in mouth position.

YOU DO
- Have each student read one line of vowel sounds on the practice page. The student should point to each letter while saying its sound. (Call on students in random order so they don't practice or rehearse their line.)

Talking Points for Professional Development:

▸ Why does the teacher use hand gestures and key words?

▸ Can the *itch* and *scratch* words cause confusion? Explain.

▸ Why would *Indian, egg*, and *elephant* not be great choices for key words?

▸ Why is it better to elongate the vowel sounds (/ăăăăăăă/) than to say them in short successions (/ă/ /ă/   /ă/)?

▸ Are all students ready to learn all five short vowel sounds in one lesson?

Notes:

• Notice that all gestures for short vowels are fluid movements, which makes it easy for the students to elongate the vowel sound as they make the movement.

• Gestures for short vowels can be better than cards on the wall for students who are trying to remember a sound. When reading, students don't have to take their eyes off the word to use a gesture, whereas they would have to look at the wall to remember a picture.

Letter-Sound Correspondence

A quick association drill can be used as a routine warm-up activity. These second-grade students who are not reading at grade level need the review to ensure accuracy and fluency with all phoneme-grapheme correspondences, including digraphs.

Lesson Component:
Letter-sound relationships.

Objective:
Students will learn a new letter-sound relationship. They will quickly produce the phoneme (sound) for the designated grapheme (letter or letter combination for a sound) when you point to the letter tile, and will quickly point to the letter tile when you articulate a given phoneme.

Materials:
- Letter tile array of all graphemes that have been learned; teacher set and student sets.
- Magnetic white boards for teacher and students.

Instructional Procedure:
- Decide which letter sounds you are going to teach. Place the appropriate tiles on teacher and student white boards.
- Say, *We are going to learn the letters that spell some sounds we already know.*
- Pick up the letter tile *t*. Say, *This letter stands for the sound /t/.* Ask students to make the motion that goes with the sound. *Say the sound when I point to the letter.* (/t/)
- Pick up the letter tile *a*. Say, *This letter stands for the sound /ă/.* Ask students to make the motion for the sound. *Say the sound when I point to the letter.* (/ă/)
- Say, *We'll review now. You point to the letter as I say the sound: /t/. You say the sound as I point to the letter.* Point to *a, a, t, a, t, t.*
- Continue with remaining consonants. Say the sound while you move the letter tile; then, ask students to say the sound when you point to the letter. Review after every new letter sound is introduced.
- Make sure every student knows the letter sounds. Check to see if each student, individually, can give you the sounds when you point to letters in random order. If a student cannot remember the sounds, make the gesture (or use the pictures) students have learned to cue the sound.

- As letters are added, do this practice drill near the beginning of each lesson, emphasizing the letters that are most difficult:

  - You say the sound; children repeat the sound and match it with the letter (grapheme) tile.

  - You point to a letter (grapheme) tile and children say the sound.

  - You say a sound, and children write the letter as they repeat the sound.

Scaffolding:

- Vary the practice. Use magnetic letters, letter-sound cards, or letter tiles.

- If a student makes an error, tell him or her the right sound and make the gesture, have everyone make the sound and gesture, and ask the student again to give the sound while pointing to the letter.

- Add about two new letter sounds per week in kindergarten; more if students are older and can learn more quickly.

Talking Points for Professional Development:

▶ Note the explanation of **digraph**. If this had been the first presentation of that concept, how would you have explained it?

▶ How important is it for students to *say* the sounds as they are finding the sounds?

▶ Practicing until all children in the group can name letter sounds quickly and accurately is very important. Does the teacher have to practice all letter sounds every day?

▶ Why is it important to practice both receptive (teacher says sound and student points to letter) and expressive (teacher points to letter and student names sound) knowledge of letter sounds?

Note:

- Notice how the teacher shows students that there are three ways to spell the sound /k/.

- Notice that it is easier for students to learn letter-sound correspondences if they have already learned the sounds and gestures in phonemic awareness lessons.

Spelling Chains

Spelling chains require students to compare one word with another and recognize the spelling for the single phoneme that has changed in the second word. This activity requires phoneme awareness, phoneme sequencing, and letter-sound association.

Lesson Component:
Spelling.

Objective:
Students will use letter tiles to change sound-spellings in dictated words, one sound at a time.

Materials:
- Teacher and student magnetic letter tiles.
- Teacher and student white boards and erasable markers.
- Lists of "chained" words (in which only one sound changes at a time).

Instructional Procedure:

I DO
- Tell students they will "chain" words by changing the spelling of one sound at a time.
- Put the needed teacher letter tiles on the board and ask students to get the appropriate letter tiles that will be used in the chain.
- Say the first word *(chum)*, finger stretch the sounds, and spell the word with tiles.
- Show students that to change the word *chum* to *bum*, you change the *ch* tile to *b*.
- Remind students that only one tile will change for each new word because only one sound changes.

WE DO
- Have students change their *ch* tile to *b*.
- Say, *Next, let's change* **bum** *to* **bump**. *What do we have to change? That's right, we add the new sound /**p**/ spelled with the letter **p** to the end. The other sounds stay the same.* Spell, then have the students touch and say the new word.
- Say, *Now change* **bump** *to* **lump**. *What sound changed? Yes, the /b/ at the beginning changed to /l/. The new word is* **lump**. Students make the word and touch and say.
- *Now change* **lump** *to* **thump**. *What sound changed? What's the new word?*

YOU DO
- Explain that you will give students the new word and they must determine what needs to be changed. Say, *Change* **thump** *to* **dump.** *What did you change?*
- Continue with the remaining words in the word chain (*damp, lamp, limp, imp, ump, rump, ramp, ram, am, at, cat, chat*).

Variation:

- Vary the practice using white boards and erasable markers. For example, write the word *tack* on your board. Ask students why the spelling for /k/ is *ck.*

- Have students write the word *tack* on their white boards.

- Ask them to change *tack* to *sack*. Either tell students the sound to change (as done with letter tiles in previous steps) or let them figure out which sound to change, depending on their ability. Writing the new word just below the old word will help students compare the subtle differences of sound and spelling.

Talking Points for Professional Development:

▸ If you start this lesson by explaining *why* we are doing it, what would that sound like?

▸ Try turning a *cat* into a *dog* by chaining. How many moves will that take?

▸ Do you use real words in chaining? What do you do with digraphs? Blends? (Digraphs are on one tile. Each sound in a blend gets its own tile.)

▸ Writing a chain is not easy because spellings may change by only one letter, but the sounds are different. It is important to prepare a chain in advance of the lesson. Why couldn't we change the word *tap* to *tar*? Why can we chain the word *chin* to *tin* when two letters change?

▸ Notice how the weaker student always watches the stronger student. The teacher could have given each student alternate turns, making sure that the weaker student got a chance to think about and process the sounds.

Phonemic Workout

A thorough phonics lesson begins with reference to speech sounds. Here, phoneme awareness is integrated into the beginning of a complete phonics lesson. Only a few minutes are needed for this beneficial activity.

Lesson Component:

Phoneme segmentation.

Objective:

Students will segment two and three sounds in simple words with the "stretch and say" technique.

Materials:

Words with two and three phonemes.

Instructional Procedure:

I DO
- Explain that the lesson will begin with a sound workout and that hearing sounds is necessary for reading and writing words.
- Say a word.
- Say the separate phonemes in the word while holding up one finger for each sound.

WE DO
- Ask students to segment more words with you.

YOU DO
- Call on individual students to segment a word.

Talking Points for Professional Development:

▸ Note the amount of time for each segment of this series. Is it necessary to spend a *lot* of time on each step?

▸ Why is this a beneficial activity even when students are learning to read with letters?

▸ The teacher gives students words with both long and short vowels for them to segment. Why does he include both long and short vowels when students are learning to read words with short vowels only?

Introducing New Letter Sounds

New letter sounds should be introduced a few at a time and practiced repeatedly in subsequent lessons. A vowel and a few consonants can be introduced in beginning lessons. These will be used right away to build simple words.

Lesson Component:
Alphabetic principle.

Objective:
Students will learn new letter-sound correspondences.

Materials:
- Magnetic teacher letter tiles and white board.
- Student tiles (pre-selected) and white boards with erasable markers.
- Vowels can be red to distinguish them from consonants, which are black.

Instructional Procedure:

I DO
- Hand out letter tiles and white boards to students. Tell them that they will be learning new letter sounds and using them to make words.
- Review known letter sounds. Ask why some letters are red (they are vowels) and others are black (they are consonants).
- Tell students the sound that each new letter represents, recalling the gesture or key word that goes with that sound.

WE DO
- Point to a letter and ask students to make the sound it represents while they move the tile to the middle of their boards.
- Dictate a sound, then have students decide with you which letter to move to the middle of their boards. Use learned gestures and key words if students fail to remember sounds or if they confuse sounds.
- Dictate a sound, then have students write the correct letter on their boards.

YOU DO
- Check with individual students by pointing to a letter, having them make the sound, and asking them to find the letter tile that goes with the sound you dictate.

Talking Points for Professional Development:

▸ While viewing this series, note how the teacher introduces and models each new concept/activity, guides practice, and encourages independent practice.

▸ Note that only a few new letters/sounds are introduced at a time.

▸ The teacher points out whether letters are vowels or consonants. Why is this important for students to know?

▸ Notice that the teacher helps the students to minimize the /uh/ when they articulate the /g/ sound.

▸ Could the students benefit from learning that vowels and consonants are terms that can describe both sounds and letters?

Building Real Words

Now the students are ready to build words with the letter-sounds they know. Model, lead, and give guided practice.

Lesson Component:
Beginning phonics.

Objective:
Students will build new words with known letter sounds.

Materials:
- Magnetic teacher letter tiles and white board with erasable marker.
- Student white boards, with letter tiles taught to date. Vowels can be red to distinguish them from consonants (black).
- List of words that can be created using target letters (include previous learned letters, if applicable). For example, if the letters are *m, s, t, f, b, a,* and *i,* the word list could be real words *at, mat, Sam, sat, sit, Tim, fit, if, bit, bat, fib, tab* and nonsense words *tam, fab, sab, mib, sib.*

Instructional Procedure:
Set Up
- Hand out letter tiles and white boards to students. Tell students they will be reviewing their letter sounds and using them to make words.

Letter-Sound Review
- Review known letter sounds. Ask students to point to a letter, tell you the name of the letter, and make the sound it represents.

> **I DO**
> - Explain to students that you can put letters together to make words if you know the sounds in the word and the letters that spell the sounds. Show them the steps to build a word:
>   - Say a word, *at.*
>   - Stretch the sounds in the word, /ă/ /t/.
>   - Draw a line for each sound in the word. (two lines.)
>   - Pull a letter tile down for each sound, saying the sound while placing the letter on a line (pull down letter tile *a,* say /ă/ while placing the letter on the line; continues with the *t* letter tile).
>   - Using touch and say, touch each tile while saying the sound, then sweep the finger under the tiles from left to right while reading the word.
>   - Put each tile away, saying the sound as the tile is placed back on the white board.

- Build the word *fit* with students.
  - Say the word, *fit*.
  - Have students repeat the word.
  - Stretch sounds in the word (/f/ /ĭ/ /t/).
  - With students, draw a line on a white board for each sound in the word. (Three lines.)
  - With students, pull a letter tile down for each sound, saying the sound as you place the letter on the line (pull down letter tile *f*, say /f/ while placing the letter on the line; continues with letter tiles *i* and *t*.

WE DO
  - Using touch and say, touch each tile while saying the sound, then sweep your finger under the tiles from left to right while reading the word.
  - Name a sound and ask students to put each tile away. This can be done in any order. Or you can call on a student to say the sound while all students place the tile back on the white board.
- Practice with a few more words on your list.

YOU DO
- Give a word to each student. Ask students to say and stretch the word and then build it with letter tiles.

Talking Points for Professional Development:

▶ When modeling and practicing new words with students who may have a learning disability or may have cognitive challenges, you may need to back up a step and use only one new sound/letter in each word. You might need to practice building several words with each new sound/letter before introducing a new sound/letter.

▶ Word choice: When selecting words for initial instruction, try to select words in the student's known vocabulary or words that the student *owns*. If introducing a word that is in the known or unknown vocabulary, provide a brief context or definition for these less familiar words. Note students' responses when the word *cot* is defined. For English Language Learner (ELL) students, don't assume knowledge, but provide context and brief definitions for the vast majority of words.

▶ Occassionally have students build nonsense words to make sure they are not memorizing the real words. Nonsense words can be syllables in longer words that they may encounter later; for example, *fash* will later be read in *fashion*.

Nonsense Words

Nonsense syllable practice is appropriate when students have practiced using the letter-sound combinations in words they know. Nonsense syllables usually recur later in real words. However, students should identify when words do and don't make sense when reading real and nonsense words in the same lesson.

Lesson Component:
Phonic decoding.

Objective:
Students will recognize that even when a word has no meaning or is unfamiliar, it can be sounded out.

Materials:
- Magnetic teacher letter tiles for known letter sounds.
- Student white boards, with same letters on them.
- Dry-erase markers and erasers.
- Teacher lists: "Martian" words (nonsense syllables with the sounds students know).

Instructional Procedure:

I DO
- Explain the concept of a nonsense word. Say, *Martians are imaginary Extra Terrestrial beings who might live in outer space on Mars. We call the words we will be reading today "Martian" words because we don't know what they mean, but a Martian might know their meaning. We can read Martian words, but we don't know what they mean. They might be nonsense words to us, but we can still read them.*
- Demonstrate building Martian words, such as *pog*, with letter tiles.
- Use the building words procedure from Demonstration 7.

WE DO
- Build Martian words together with students: *fam, tib.*

YOU DO
- Give students the following words to build: *fap, jom, cug, ret, zid.*

Talking Points for Professional Development:

▸ Discuss whether or not this step should be included with your ELL population.

▸ It is important to be able to read nonsense words for three primary reasons: (1) Reading them shows that students know how to decode words and haven't just memorized them; (2) nonsense words are often part of multisyllabic words that students need to decode; and (3) real words that are not in a student's vocabulary may seem like nonsense words when they are first encountered.

The "Question and Answer" Game

The game shown here helps students realize the meanings of the words they are reading and attend to both the sounds and letter patterns in the words.

Lesson Component:
Automatic (fluent) recognition of decodable words.

Objective:
Students will locate a word in a list of decodable words in response to meaning cues.

Materials:
- List (or index cards) of words that have been decoded or spelled previously.
- Teacher's list of questions to ask about the words.

Instructional Procedure:
- Read the word cards with students to ensure that they can recognize the words.
- Say, *I'll ask a question about the words on these cards. When you find the word, pick it up.* Ask questions such as:

    *Which word means the opposite of **out**?* (In.)

    Find a word for an animal that gives us pork. (Pig.)

    What do you wipe dust from furniture with? (Rag.)

    *Find a word that rhymes with **sock**.* (Dock.)

Note: Keep the pace lively. This is a drill for automatic word recognition.

Talking Points for Professional Development:

▶ When words are introduced in the beginning, a brief meaning discussion would be helpful, especially with ELL students.

▶ With ELL students, you would not want to mix real words with nonsense words for this activity.

Reading Word Patterns

The English spelling system includes many recurring letter sequences that form whole syllables or parts of syllables. These are also known as "phonograms," "word families," or "rime patterns."

Lesson Component:

Automatic word reading.

Objective:

Students will automatically and accurately read words with common rime patterns.

Materials:

- List of sound/spellings and rime patterns that have been taught.
- Several lists of words that share a rime (*old*, *cold*, *mold*, *sold*, *told*; *map*, *sap*, *rap*, *cap*, and *gap*).
- Student sheet with three to five columns of "family" words, each of which includes a "ringer"—one odd word that does not follow the pattern.

Instructional Procedure:

- Explain that this game has two objectives: reading all the words in a column accurately and quickly, and finding the word that does not follow the pattern.
- Present word lists with family words and "ringers," words that don't not follow the rime pattern.
- A student reads the words aloud. After reading all the words in the column, the student names the "ringer."
- If the student misses the ringer, ask him or her to reread each word aloud, pointing to each word.
- If the student does not find the ringer the second time, have the student name the letters that are the same in every word, then point to and read the word that is different. Have the student read the list again.

Talking Points for Professional Development:

▶ The teacher uses the word "ringer" for the oddball word. Is it sufficiently defined here?

▶ Why include a ringer in the list of words that have the same pattern?

▶ Some reading programs begin reading instruction by teaching word families instead of phonemes. Why might this cause confusion for some students?

Reading Nonsense Words

This brief drill builds fluency in phonic decoding. Students should know the sound-symbol correspondences so well that blending whole syllables becomes easy.

Lesson Component:
Phonic decoding fluency.

Objective:
Students will automatically and accurately read nonsense words with a CVC pattern.

Materials:
- A list of nonsense syllables. These should have been taught and practiced in earlier parts of the lesson.
- Timer or stopwatch

Instructional Procedure:
- Pass out word lists to each student. Tell students that these are "Martian," or nonsense, words.
- Have students work in pairs.
- Appoint one student to be the Reader and another to be the Timer.
- The Timer records the time and number of errors for each reading as the Reader reads the words. Have the Reader read again to try to improve his or her time and eliminate errors. Finally, have the Reader read a third time if he or she makes errors on the second reading.
- Repeat the process with students changing roles.

mog	gog	tig	tog	som
gom	pog	mog	gom	rog
fim	mig	fam	mag	rin
pom	rin	nam	nop	fom

Alternate Procedure:
- Give students a list of nonsense syllables organized in five columns.
- Call on each student to read one column or one row of words.

Talking Points for Professional Development:

▶ Note how the teacher is specific in his reinforcement of the last student who decoded and blended his nonsense word.

Fluency Builder

This part of the lesson provides practice reading whole words whose letter-sound correspondences are known and predictable.

Lesson Component:
Fluency in word recognition.

Objective:
Students will read regular words as wholes.

Materials:
- Student list with three columns of 10–20 words that use the letter-sound correspondences that have been taught. The same words are in each column, arranged differently.
- Timer or stopwatch.
- Teacher recording sheet with word lists and writing space for time and error notations.

Instructional Procedure:
- Students work in pairs.
- Explain that this exercise is to practice reading whole words with letter sounds students know.
- One student reads the words in the first column without timing. (The first column of words is used to ensure accuracy.) The other student checks for errors.
- The student's partner times as the student reads the words in the next two columns.
- Students record time and errors for each column. Note errors students make and reteach those sound-spelling correspondences in the next lesson.
- Error correction: After the student finishes reading the first column, point to any words that he or she misread. Have the student touch and say the letter sounds in that word and read it again. If the student misreads the word again, touch and say and read the word, then have the student imitate what you did.

Talking Points for Professional Development:

▶ Encourage your students to chart their progress with fluency builders.

▶ It is important to correct any errors during the first reading, which is not timed, so that students read accurately when they are timed. Always teach accuracy before speed.

▶ Why is it important to allow students to read the words three times?

Reading Sentences

Students who have learned to decode words using phonics need varying amounts of practice reading phrases, sentences, and passages or books with examples of words that contain those correspondences. Phrases, sentences, and passages should include heart words already studied.

Lesson Component:

Supported reading of decodable text.

Objective:

Students will read and comprehend sentences with decodable words and heart words.

Materials:

- Pocket chart for sentence strips.
- Ten sentences that include decodable and heart words, written on sentence strips.
- *Or,* individual practice sheets for student reading.

Instructional Procedure:

- Lay the sentence strips on the table or place them in a pocket chart.
- Ask individual students to select a sentence and read it aloud. Ask the student a question about the sentence before moving on to the next student. For example, ask *What could Tim be?* about the sentence "Tim is not a pig."

Alternate Procedure:

- Use sentences that can be sequenced into a simple story. Mix up the sentence strips, and ask students to read them one-by-one.
- Ask the group to find the sentence that should come first, second, third, and so forth. Arrange the sentences in order and ask the group or individuals to read the whole story.

Alternate Activity: Phrase and Sentence Reading

Instructional Procedure:

- Place four to five phrases (on sentence strips) with three to six known words apiece in the pocket chart.
- Model the prosody, or voice contour, of phrase reading as you sweep your hand under the words.
- Read the phrases chorally with students. Call on individuals to read phrases in random order.

- Play a question and answer game, asking questions such as *Which group of words is about two animals?* (A pig and a ram.)
- Give students about ten phrases to practice reading aloud with a partner. Call on individuals to model "natural" phrasing.

Alternative Activity: Scrambled Sentences (Sentence Anagrams)

Instructional Procedure:
- Give each student an envelope containing individual words that can be arranged into a sentence. The first word should begin with a capital letter, and the last word should have a period after it.
- Have each student arrange the words in his or her envelope into a sentence.
- Have each student read his or her sentence aloud.
- Students can put their words back into the envelope and exchange envelopes, arranging and reading the sentences again.

Talking Points for Professional Development:

▸ Note how the teacher encourages students to read their sentences silently first before oral reading.

▸ Note how the teacher models and encourages proper expression and fluency when practicing sentences.

▸ How does the scrambled-sentences activity help students develop awareness of English syntax?

Dictation

Spelling is the inverse of reading. (When reading, we see letters or letter clusters and match them to sounds. When spelling, we know the sounds and select the letters that match the sounds.) Dictation helps students develop habits for spelling common words and word patterns. Students who can recall words automatically during writing are more likely to write longer and better organized compositions than students who do not know the spellings of common words.

Lesson Component:
Spelling and sentence writing.

Objective:
Students will write and then monitor the correctness of regular and irregular words in dictated sentences.

Materials:
- List of three to five sounds, three to five words with letter-sound relationships already taught, and two to three heart words to dictate.
- List of two to three sentences to dictate that use the heart words and words with letter sounds already taught.
- White board or chalkboard for the teacher.
- Paper and pencil for each student.

Instructional Procedure:
- Warm up by dictating a few sounds, pattern words, and irregular words that will be used in the sentences.
- Ask students to repeat the sound or word before they write it.
- Dictate the first sentence for students.
- Ask students to repeat the sentence before they write it. This ensures that the students correctly heard the dictation and reinforces memory for words.
- Have students write what was dictated.
- Have one student read the sentence while everyone checks for accurate spelling and puctuation. Students can make changes at this point.
- Show the sentence on the board.
- Have students check and correct their work by looking at the correctly written sentence on the board.
- Repeat the procedure for a second or third sentence.

Alternate Activity: Sentence Anagrams With Writing

Materials:

- Student worksheets with mixed-up sentences ready to cut up and rearrange or envelopes with words already cut up.
- Scissors.
- Paper with spaces for students to paste words in rearranged sentences, with lines underneath for writing the words.
- Paper and pencil for students to use for writing.

Instructional Procedure:

- Prepare by having students cut apart the words, or give them envelopes with a set of word cards for each mixed-up sentence.
- Ask students to arrange their words into a sentence.
- Ask each student to read the sentence aloud, pointing to each word as they read it.
- Get out lined paper and pencils.
- Have students write the sentence on their paper and check it for spelling, capitalization, and punctuation.
- Practice the activity again with the second and third scrambled sentence.

Talking Points for Professional Development:

▶ Note how the teacher becomes more and more relaxed and animated as he progresses through this lesson. His comfort with the group transfers to students, and he encourages them to take more risks.

▶ Note how the teacher, early in the lesson, encourages students to ask what something means if they don't know. Later in the lesson, students had permission to ask for clarification. In several subsequent lessons, students have asked for clarifications and have always been positively reinforced for doing so.

▶ If one word is capitalized and another has a period, would that help students create a sentence?

Reading Decodable Books

Decodable texts afford students the opportunity to practice using the letter-sound correspondences and heart words they have been taught in earlier parts of the lesson. Decodable texts can be read using comprehension strategies, just like any other text. See Appendix H for a list of decodable texts.

Lesson Component:
Supported reading.

Objective:
Students will read and comprehend books with decodable words and heart words that have been previously taught.

Materials:
- Decodable book with standard book structure (title, author, illustrations, etc.).

Instructional Procedure:
- Preview the book briefly:
  - Ask students to find the title on the title page.
  - Ask students to point to the author's name. Read the author's name to students.
  - Ask students to browse the book for a minute before reading to find out what it might be about. Solicit a few comments that predict what the story is about.
  - Ask students to think of a question they might find the answer to if they read the book.
- Read aloud, using one of the following techniques:
  - Individual, unsynchronized reading aloud. Everyone reads at their own pace but tracks where they are with their finger so the teacher knows where they are.
  - Choral reading. Everyone reads together as one voice.
  - Choral and solo reading. The group reads a page together, then individual students read a page. Repeat.
  - Silent reading of identified sections, followed by one person reading the section aloud.
  - Partner reading. Student #1 reads the book or a part of the book first, and student #2 follows along, helping with unknown words. Then, student #2 asks student #1 to tell what the story was about. Roles are then reversed.

- After reading, check comprehension by:
  - Asking a student to retell the story.
  - Asking a student to connect the story topic to the student's own experience (or helping students connect the story to their own experiences).
  - Clarifying and using any new words whose meanings were not known.
  - Modeling more natural expression and phrasing and having students read after you model.

Talking Points for Professional Development:

▸ Note that the final part of the lesson is not just decoding the text, but gathering meaning or comprehension from the passage.

▸ Although accurate reading is the main purpose of using decodable books, comprehension, fluency, vocabulary, and oral expression can also be taught using decodable readers.

Word Sorting With -*ck*

Word sorting helps students look closely at orthographic patterns. In this word sorting demonstration, students need a considerable amount of teacher support just to see where the target spelling is in the example words. They learn that -*ck* always occurs at the end of the word.

Lesson Component:

Phonics and spelling.

Objective:

Students will recognize and spell a sound that has more than one spelling. In this demonstration the choice is when to use -*ck* as opposed to *c* or *k*.

Materials:

- Pocket chart or magnetic board.
- Cards or magnetic tiles with various spellings for a target sound (e.g., *c, k, -ck*).
- Word cards with four to six examples of each spelling pattern (e.g., *cup, shuck, kit, cot, sock, Ken, cab, tack, kid*).

Instructional Procedure:

I DO
- Say, *Some sounds are spelled different ways. We're going to learn a pattern for spelling /**k**/.*
- Remind students that the sound /k/ can be spelled three different ways: *c, k,* and *ck*. (Do not teach the less common *ch* (*chorus*) or *que* (*antique*) patterns in this lesson.)
- Place the *c, k,* and *ck* grapheme cards at the top of the pocket chart or on the table so that each card is at the top of a column.
- Tell students that you will show them some words, and they will tell you how the sound /k/ is spelled in each.
- Demonstrate by reading one word with each spelling (e.g., *cub, kit, duck*).
- Place the word under the appropriate spelling in the pocket chart or on the table.

WE DO
- Hold up word cards, asking students to read each card and then tell you which column the word belongs in.
- Help students identify and verbalize the presence of the target spelling pattern.

- Give each student three or four cards to sort into columns.
- Discovery of the pattern: Once all cards are on the chart, tell students that there is a pattern. Ask students if they can figure out the pattern.
- Talk through the pattern to make sure students understand. For students who need to learn patterns in small doses, point out that -ck is used at the end of words in this lesson. In another lesson, teach them that:

  YOU DO

  - We use c to spell /k/ when /k/ is followed by the letters a, o, or u.

  - We use k to spell /k/ when /k/ is followed by the letters e or i.

  - We usually use c to spell /k/ when /k/ is followed by another consonant sound.

Talking Points for Professional Development:

▶ How does using Martian words impact the activity?

▶ What steps are used to scaffold this instruction?

▶ Why doesn't the teacher press students to see that -ck is always used after a short vowel?

Consonant Blends

Students benefit from explicit teaching of the difference between consonant blends and consonant digraphs (two letters that stand for one speech sound).

Lesson Component:
Phonic decoding.

Objective:
Students will read short vowel words with consonant blends and digraphs.

Materials:
- Large magnetic letter tiles that include digraphs.
- Teacher lists:
    - Words for phonemic workout.
    - Real words for students to build.
    - Martian words for students to build.
- Word cards.
- Questions for word cards.
- Student white boards and tiles.
- Worksheet with list of ten to fifteen words with digraphs and blends.

Instructional Procedure:

I DO

- Explain the concept of blends as two consonants next to each other that spell two consonant sounds. Use letter tiles to build the word *best* after stretching the sounds on your fingers. Point out that there are four phonemes and four letters. The letters *s* and *t* are consonant letters spelling consonant sounds that happen to be next to each other.

- Use letter tiles to build the word *black* after stretching the sounds on your fingers. Point out that there are four phonemes and five letters because the digraph **ck** is needed to spell the phoneme /k/ at the end of the word after the vowel. Review that a digraph is two letters that spell one phoneme, whereas a blend is just two consonants next to each other, each spelling a separate phoneme. Show that with the blend **bl** in *black* we can take away one letter and the remaining letter still spells the same phoneme it did before: *black* to *back* or *black* to *lack*.

WE DO
- Build several more words with students, identifying the blends and digraphs in each word. Have students, with support and modeling, use letter tiles to build words such as *shelf*, *crash*, *chest*, *fresh*, and *thump*.

YOU DO
- Have students read individual words, underlining the words that spell each sound. Digraphs are underlined with one continuous line. Blends have each letter underlined separately.
- *Or*, have students read words from word cards and tell which letters are blends and which are digraphs.

Talking Points for Professional Development:

▶ Note how the teacher starts with what is known and then builds from there.

▶ Note how the teacher restates the directions before he expects students to respond.

▶ The teacher can keep all students involved when he's focusing on one student by having all students build and whisper, or ghost talk, while the *target* student is verbalizing out loud.

▶ What is the best order for presentation of blends? Initial? Final?

▶ Common blends without /r/, /l/, or nasals, such as *st-* or *-st,* should be targeted first.

Alternate Oral Reading

Alternate oral reading in a small group affords the teacher a chance to hear each student read aloud. All students should be following the text and should be ready to participate in the discussion of the text's meaning.

Lesson Component:
Supported text reading.

Objective:
Students will read and comprehend books at their instructional level (the level at which 95%–97% of the words are decodable, and in the students' vocabulary).

Materials:
- Appealing text with 95%–97% known words.

Instructional Procedure:
- Preview the book briefly.
  - Ask students to find the book's title on the title page.
  - Ask students to find the author's name. Read the author's name to them.
  - Ask students to browse the book for several seconds before reading to find out what it might be about. Solicit a few comments that predict what the story is about.
  - Ask students to think of a question they might find the answer to if they read the book.
  - Preview any difficult or new vocabulary.
- Read aloud.
  - One student reads and the others follow along. Encourage finger-point tracking.
- During and after reading, check comprehension by:
  - Asking a student to retell what has happened.
  - Asking a student to predict what will happen next.
  - Asking a student to connect the story topic to the student's own experience (or help students connect the story to their own experiences).
  - Clarifying and using any new words whose meanings were not known.
  - Supplying more natural expression and phrasing.

Correction Procedure:

- If a student does not know a word, encourage this three-step strategy:

  - Look for letter sounds and word parts you know.

  - Sound the word out. (Use touch and say, if necessary.)

  - After the word is sounded out, check the word's use in the sentence for sense.

Talking Points for Professional Development:

▶ What preview techniques are used?

▶ How does the teacher keep students engaged with the comprehension while working on decoding and fluent reading?

Choral Reading

Choral reading is another form of oral reading practice that most children enjoy because other group members provide support for accuracy and fluency.

Lesson Component:
Supported text reading.

Objective:
Students will read and comprehend books at their instructional level (that level at which 95%–97% of the words are known).

Materials:
Appealing text with 95%–97% known words.

Instructional Procedure:
- Preview the book briefly.
  - Ask students to find the book's title on the title page.
  - Ask students to find the author's name. Read the author's name to them.
  - Ask students to browse the book for several seconds before reading to find out what it might be about. Solicit a few comments that predict what the story is about.
  - Ask students to think of a question they might find the answer to if they read the book.
  - Preview any difficult or new vocabulary.
- Read aloud.
  - Students read aloud together. To synchronize reading, ask students to begin when you give the signal. Students should track text with their fingers.
- During and after reading, check comprehension by:
  - Asking a student to retell what has happened.
  - Asking a student to predict what will happen next.
  - Connect the story topic to the student's own experience (or help students connect story to their own experiences).
  - Clarifying and using any new words whose meanings were not known.
  - Supplying more natural expression and phrasing.

Correction Procedure:

If a student does not know a word, encourage this three-step strategy:

- Look for letter sounds and word parts you know.
- Sound the word out. (Use touch and say, if necessary.)
- After the word is sounded out, check the word's use in the sentence for sense.

Talking Points for Professional Development:

▸ What does the teacher do to support the reading?

▸ When she starts the lesson, what is her focus? Why do you think she starts that way?

▸ How does she support students when they struggle with decoding?

Word Recognition Strategy

Poor readers tend to rely too much on context and pictures to guess at words. This is because sounding words out takes effort, especially for students with weak phonological skills. Guessing becomes less reliable as fewer pictures accompany text and as words become more difficult. Therefore, in the early stages of reading and during remediation it is critical that novice or poor readers develop the habit of reading every word accurately. This is done by sounding out unfamiliar words and then checking to see if the word makes sense. When a student misreads a word, the teacher has the student look at the letters and sound out the word as the first strategy for reading the word. Only after the student has decoded the word accurately does he or she check context to determine whether the word makes sense.

In this reading lesson, third-grade students who are well below benchmark on DIBELS ORF find the text challenging. Their lack of fluency in applying basic phonics skills is evident.

Lesson Component:
Supported text reading.

Objective:
Students will try to sound out unknown words before appealing to context for the word's identity.

Materials:
Appealing text at the students' instructional level.

Instructional Procedure:
- Tell students to use the following three-step strategy when they come to a word they don't know:
  - Look for letter sounds and word parts you know.
  - Sound the word out. (Use touch and say, if necessary.)
  - After the word is sounded out, check the word's use in the sentence for sense.
- Begin reading aloud. Coach students through the process above when they come to a word they do not know.
- If necessary, model sound-by-sound blending (touch and say), and then ask the student to sound out the word.

Talking Points for Professional Development:

▶ Note how the teacher continues to state what students are doing correctly.

▶ The teacher helps a student gain better fluency by inviting the other students to read. This is after a longer decoding passage, so it also re-engages the other students. How else can a teacher help a student who struggles more than the rest of the class?

▶ How does the teacher gradually change so that students gain more independence with using the strategy.

▶ How does the teacher conclude the lesson?

Phrasing

Phrase reading improves fluency. After students have been taught the individual words or phonic patterns in a passage, they benefit from a model of smooth, expressive reading that conveys the meaning of the connected text. Scooping under words in a phrase, marking phrase boundaries, or simply rereading with better phrasing are all helpful techniques. Here, the technique is modeled with second graders who have already learned basic reading skills.

Lesson Component:

Reading fluency.

Objective:

Students will read with natural and expressive phrasing.

Materials:

- Appealing books that are well within the students' difficulty level (90%–95% correct).
- Index cards.

Instructional Procedure:

I DO
- Write several phrases on index cards.
- Explain that students will practice reading phrases in the same way that they talk.
- Using one of the phrases on cards, model the difference between reading a phrase word by word and reading it with expression.

WE DO
- Have students read one of the phrases on the index card after you read it.

YOU DO
- Give each of the students two or three word cards with phrases on them.
- Have the students read the phrases on their cards.
- If a student reads disfluently, help him or her read with fluency by modeling how to read the phrase and having him or her read after you have modeled.

Alternate Procedure:

- Introduce a book in which you have marked off phrases with a pencil, or introduce a typed sheet in which phrase boundaries are marked in the sentences.
- Scoop under phrases with your finger or an eraser, modeling and practicing with students using a "natural" sounding voice.

- Ask individual students to read from the book. When a student reads without good phrasing, use the eraser end of your pencil to scoop under the words in the phrase while you model a better way to read the phrase, then ask the student to read the phrase again. Praise the student when you note improvement.

Prompts:

- Say, *Make it sound like real talking.*
- Say, *Read it smoothly.*

Talking Points for Professional Development:

▸ How does the teacher explain what the activity will be before starting?

▸ How does the teacher use her voice tone to reinforce students?

▸ How does the teacher reinforce what the student did correctly?

▸ How does the teacher help students prepare for the phrases they will encounter in the reading?

▸ Would using a swooping motion under the words instead of tapping each word make a difference in reading fluency?

Partner Reading

Peer-assisted learning has strong research validation. This technique enables the teacher to work with one student while peer partners coach each other through book reading. The roles of coach and reader are assigned, modeled, practiced, and then carried out independently.

Lesson Component:
Reading fluency.

Objective:
Students will read text with accuracy, fluency, and expression.

Materials:
- Several books or stories that students have read in previous lessons.
- Partner reading prompt cards (coach, reader).

Instructional Procedure:

I DO
- Select several books or stories for students to read that are at their instructional level.
- Model the following process using a student as your partner:
  - Sit side-by-side so a book can be shared between two readers.
  - Assign one person the role of coach and the other the role of reader.
  - The reader selects a book to read. As the reader reads, the coach follows along and watches for any mistakes. The coach then either supplies the correct word or asks the reader to try again.
  - After the book is read, model a comprehension check in which the coach asks the reader to tell "what happened" on each page as the book is reviewed.

WE DO
- Exchange roles with the student; she becomes the coach, and you become the reader.
- Make a mistake, and elicit the correction response from the coach, while the other students watch.
- Role play the comprehension check while the other students watch.

YOU DO
- Have students work in pairs, assigning coach and reader cards initially. Check book or story choices.
- Have coach and reader teams continue switching roles, reading books and doing comprehension checks.

Prompts:

- If the reader reads a word incorrectly, the coach may say, *Check that word* before supplying the word.

- The coach may say, *That word is _____. Say the word.* Have the reader repeat the word before going on.

Note: This partner-reading format is adapted from Mathes, Torgesen, Allen, & Allor (2001). *First-Grade PALS (Peer-Assisted Learning Strategies)*. Longmont, CO: Sopris West.

Talking Points for Professional Development:

▶ What makes this an effective lesson?

▶ How does the teacher model the activities?

▶ Note how the teacher states what students are doing correctly.

Fluency Practice

Once students read enough individual words with sufficient accuracy, they need to practice reading them in connected text. Two techniques for building reading fluency demonstrated with second graders are simultaneous oral reading and alternate oral reading.

Lesson Component:
Reading fluency.

Objective:
Students will read with sufficient fluency to support comprehension.

Materials:
- Text at the student's instructional or independent reading level.

Instructional Procedure—Simultaneous Oral Reading:
- Offer students several books within their instructional reading levels and ask each student to select one.
- Sit side-by-side with one student. Explain that you will be practicing reading smoothly and with a little more speed.
- Read simultaneously with the student as you track the text with your finger or pencil, leading the student to read a bit faster.
- Model fluent reading of a passage, and then ask the student to read the passage the same way you did.
- Use your finger to track the text slightly ahead of the student's reading, encouraging the student to read the words more quickly.

Note: This student reads quite well for second grade, and only limited practice of this kind with this student is necessary.

Instructional Procedure—Alternate Oral Reading:
- Offer students several books within their instructional reading levels and ask each student to select one.
- Sit side-by-side with one student. Explain that you will each take turns reading one page (or paragraph) at a time. The student should track your reading with his or her finger. You will track the student's reading with your finger.

- If the student misreads any word, wait until after he has finished his part and have him read the sentence with the misread word again, tracking with his finger as he reads. If he misreads the word again, use the following procedure to help him decode the word:

  - Look for letter sounds and word parts you know.

  - Sound the word out. (Use touch and say, if necessary.)

  - After the word is sounded out, check the word's use in the sentence for sense.

Talking Points for Professional Development:

▸ What two techniques does the teacher use to make certain the student knows the words in the upcoming text?

▸ Does the teacher model and give strategies for increasing speed? Where and how?

Alternate Activity: Repeated Reading

Lesson Component:
Reading fluency.

Objective:
Students will increase fluency in connected text reading.

Materials:
- Books or passages at the student's instructional reading level (90%–95% of words known).
- Timer or stopwatches.
- Chart for recording time and fluency (words correct per minute) after each reading.

Instructional Procedure
- Briefly preview the topic of the book or passage that is to be read.
- Ask the student to read the passage aloud. Tell the student you will ask him or her to tell you about the passage.
- Start the stopwatch; when 60 seconds are up, mark the last word the student read.
- Ask the student to tell you as much as he or she can about the passage to check comprehension.
- Chart the words correct per minute (total words read in 60 seconds minus words read incorrectly) and point out any word reading errors that should be corrected.
- Ask the student to practice reading the passage several more times by him or herself. Practice can also be done with a tape recorder or with a partner who can help with unknown words.
- The next day, time the student in a one-minute reading of the same passage and again record words correct per minute.
- Repeat this procedure one more time. After three timed readings of the same passage, move on to another.

Supported Group Writing

Even with rudimentary skills, students can be led through the first steps in composing and writing a sentence in a small group.

Lesson Component:
Supported writing.

Objective:
Students will participate in writing complete sentences, using skills they have learned.

Materials:
- Chart and easel.
- Markers—various colors and black.
- One-inch correction tape.

Instructional Procedure:
- Ask one student to compose an oral sentence about a book that the group has read recently. Help the student, if necessary, to complete a clearly and correctly worded sentence.
- Ask the group to repeat the sentence three times to remember it.
- Give each student a different color marker.
- Each student will write a part of the sentence on the chart. Each student's contribution to the writing on the chart can be tracked by color. Use the black marker for parts that students cannot write, and model the process of thinking through the spellings and punctuation.

Talking Points for Professional Development:
▸ When the teacher asks students to remember the sentence, how does she have them practice?

▸ What makes supported writing an integral step in the overall lesson?

▸ How could this activity be adapted to support ELL oral language instruction?

Supported Independent Writing

Students should regularly apply the spelling, punctuation, handwriting, and sentence composition skills they have learned. At this point, they should be independent enough to attempt sentence writing. Accurate transcription is emphasized even though writers are working independently with support.

Lesson Component:
Supported writing.

Objective:
Students will compose and write complete sentences, using skills they have learned.

Materials:
- Student journals or lined paper.
- Practice paper for experimenting with spelling.
- Pencils or fine-point markers.
- One-inch correction tape.

Instructional Procedure:
- Pass out students' journals or paper. Ask students to put their names and headings on the paper.
- In response to a question you ask about a book just read, have one student orally create a sentence about the book.
- Ask students to recite the sentence three times, in different voices.
- Ask students to write the sentence on their papers. *All students will write the same sentence.* Use correction tape when students make errors.
- When errors occur, correct them immediately by re-teaching the spelling pattern, using sound boxes for spelling or spelling by analogy to a known word. Tell students any patterns or irregular words they have not yet been taught.
- Have students check their own sentences by writing the correct sentence on a chart, if necessary.

Talking Points for Professional Development:
▶ When the first student finally gets the sentence the way the teacher wants it, how does the teacher capitalize on the student's success?
▶ Are students able to generalize from the simple sentence to creating expanded sentences?

Comprehensive Lesson: Reading Decodable Text

In this segment, we show an entire 34-minute lesson taught by Judi Dodson to a group of novice readers in first grade. To prepare this lesson, Judi used a decodable text with a high proportion of short *i* words. The lesson flows together seamlessly, although segments can be identified, as noted below.

Lesson Component:

Fluent reading of decodable text.

Objective:

Students will read a previously unseen text with learned phonic patterns and heart words.

Materials:

- Books with decodable text for each student.
- "Realia" for illustrating vocabulary words.
- Letter tiles and markers for white board spelling.
- Paper and pencil for each student.

Lesson Segments:

- Phoneme Awareness
- Building and Decoding Words With Letter Tiles
- Vocabulary Development
- Before Reading
- During Reading
- After Reading
- Writing

Talking Points for Professional Development:

▶ How does the teacher use her voice (softening) and her posture to engage and keep students' attention?

▶ What does the teacher do to "prime" the group for each step of the lesson?

▶ Note how the teacher uses props to give multisensory instruction.

▶ Where do you see the teacher using "I do, We do, You do"?

▶ How smoothly does the teacher transition through the scaffolding steps? What aids those transitions?

▶ Note how the teacher allows the students to manipulate and play briefly with toys/tools before she attempts instruction.

Part 4: Teaching Advanced Phonics

What is advanced phonics instruction?

Advanced phonics instruction begins after students can read one-syllable words with short vowels, blends, and digraphs. The main focus of advanced phonics lessons is teaching sounds that have multiple spellings, such as the long vowels and /er/. Advanced phonics also includes reading multisyllabic words and words with common prefixes and suffixes. Advanced phonics should lead to analysis of meaningful word parts (morphology).

Who needs advanced phonics instruction?

Many reading programs begin advanced phonics instruction toward the end of first grade and continue it into second grade, with phonics principles reinforced through spelling instruction in grades 3 through 6. The principles demonstrated in the *Teaching Reading Essentials* lessons are incorporated in many effective reading programs.

Struggling readers who benefit from advanced phonics instruction are proficient with basic reading skills, such as CVC words, short vowel words with blends and digraphs, and the most common sight words. Such students will exhibit one or more of the following characteristics:

- Slow or inaccurate when reading multisyllable words.
- Inaccurate when reading long vowel patterns in unfamiliar words.
- Inaccurate when reading words with vowel-*r* patterns.
- Likely to omit or confuse suffixes when reading.
- Over-reliant on contextual clues to read unknown words.
- Poor spellers for their grade level.

Students at this level of instruction usually score below benchmark on the DIBELS Oral Reading Fluency (ORF) and at or above benchmark on Nonsense Word Fluency (NWF).

Why teach advanced phonics and word recognition?

Fluency in word recognition is an important goal. To this end, there is much more to know about words than one-syllable, regular, short-vowel patterns. Many students learn the basics but never become accurate or comfortable with longer words or more complex phonics patterns. Advanced phonics principles need to be taught for both word recognition and spelling. In addition, being able to read multisyllabic words with attention to each syllable is a stepping stone to recognizing meaningful word parts, or morphemes.

What is taught at this level?

- Long vowel patterns (silent *e*, vowel teams, open syllables)
- Vowel-*r* patterns
- Consonant-*le* syllables
- Diphthongs *oi, ou*
- Syllabication principles
- Meaning of inflectional suffixes (past tense, plurals, *ing*, *en*, etc.)
- Ending rules for spelling (consonant doubling, drop *e*, change *y* to *i*)
- Contractions
- Concept of base word + suffix constructions
- Schwa

For a complete overview of the content of instruction, see *Language Essentials for Teachers of Reading and Spelling* (LETRS) Module 10, *Reading Big Words: Syllabication and Advanced Decoding* (Sopris West, 2005).

How are these skills taught?

At this level, we de-emphasize techniques such as word building and touch and say (sound-by-sound blending), and we focus more on recognizing "chunks" such as long vowel patterns, syllables, and meaningful word parts (morphemes). Fluency-building and reading for meaning are given greater emphasis and more instructional time within the lesson framework. Text used during instruction should contain words the students can read with 95%–97% accuracy; that is, if students misread or misunderstand about 3–5 words in 100, the text is the right level of difficulty for instruction.

There are several parts to a comprehensive advanced phonics lesson. Not all components will be included every day; however, the following should be included every two to three lessons throughout the week.

- State the lesson objective and purpose.
- Review previously taught concepts as necessary.
- Explicitly teach the new phoneme-grapheme pattern or syllable/morpheme concept.
- Provide guided practice in decoding and spelling new words.
- Use word sorts and other practice routines that require attention to letter patterns.
- Build fluency in reading word lists, phrases, sentences, and decodable text.
- Develop prosody (the flow of reading) through oral passage reading.

DVD Navigation

<table>
<tr><th colspan="4">Part 4: Teaching Advanced Phonics</th></tr>
<tr><td colspan="4">For students who are below benchmark on DIBELS ORF.</td></tr>
<tr><th>Demonstration Video</th><th>Activity Name</th><th>Page</th><th>Time (minutes)</th></tr>
<tr><td></td><td>Introduction to Part 4</td><td></td><td>12:29</td></tr>
<tr><td colspan="4">Introducing Critical Concepts</td></tr>
<tr><td>1</td><td>Suffix -ed
    Professional Development Session</td><td>106</td><td>12:19
15:04</td></tr>
<tr><td>2</td><td>Multisyllabic Words</td><td>108</td><td>8:02</td></tr>
<tr><td>3</td><td>Understanding Schwa</td><td>110</td><td>15:17</td></tr>
<tr><td colspan="4">Vowel-Consonant-e (VCe)</td></tr>
<tr><td>4</td><td>Teaching Magic e</td><td>112</td><td>31:06</td></tr>
<tr><td colspan="4">More Syllable Patterns</td></tr>
<tr><td>5</td><td>Multisyllabic Words With Magic e</td><td>116</td><td>17:21</td></tr>
<tr><td>6</td><td>Spellings for /er/</td><td>118</td><td>13:57</td></tr>
<tr><td colspan="4">Multiple Spellings for a Long Vowel</td></tr>
<tr><td>7</td><td>Fluency: Long o</td><td>120</td><td>25:31</td></tr>
</table>

Suffix -ed

To help students understand, read, and spell words with inflections, lessons should begin with awareness of the relationship between the meaningful word part (inflectional morpheme), the syllable structure of a word, and the sound of the ending. Past tense *-ed* is especially challenging for students because it has three sounds (/t/, /d/, and /ed/) and does not always add a second syllable to the word. After exposure to the concept of *-ed* as suffix with three sounds, many students will need extended practice identifying the structure of past tense words with the suffix *-ed*. They will also need to practice spelling these words. (Some phonics programs include this instruction with basic phonics.)

Lesson Component:
Decoding and spelling words with the suffix *-ed*.

Objective:
Students will recognize and classify words by the pronunciation of the past tense suffix *-ed*.

Materials:
- Magnetic teacher letter tiles for /t/, /d/, and /ed/ and a magnetized syllable board.
- Word cards with examples of *-ed* sounding like /t/, /d/, and /ed/ (e.g., *jumped*, *sailed*, *rented*).

Instructional Procedure:

- Explain that the suffix *-ed* makes a verb into the past tense.
  – The verb is the base word, and the *ed* is the suffix.
  – For example, *rent* is a verb. *Rented* is the past tense because of the suffix *-ed*.
- The suffix *-ed* is unusual because it spells three sounds. It is always spelled the same way because its job is to tell us that the action took place before now.
- Place tiles or cards with /t/, /d/, and /ed/ on the white board. Give the sound of each and explain that each tile represents a sound that *-ed* can make.
- Put index cards with the word *rented* on the board. Read the word aloud, and use it in the sentence "I rented a boat." Have students tell you the number of syllables. (Two.) Say, *The second syllable is /**ed**/, so we put it under the /**ed**/ tile.*
  – Repeat the process with the word *sailed*, using the sentence, "I sailed a boat." (/d/). Have students tell you how many syllables. (One.) Say, *This time, we don't say /**ed**/, and we add /**d**/ to the base word.*
  – Repeat the process with the word *jumped* (one syllable), using the sentence *I jumped in the boat* (/t/).
- Tell students they can remember these three endings with the sentence "I rent*ed* a boat, jump*ed* in, and sail*ed* away."

WE DO
- Give each student a card with a past tense word on it.
- Have each student read the word, with teacher's help as needed.
- Have each student identify the base word and state the sound of the suffix -ed, with teacher's help as needed.
- Have each student sort the word under the appropriate sound for the suffix -ed.
- Have students sort cards. Individual students take turns reading the words on the cards.

YOU DO
- Have students read and sort words on their own with word cards, or have them write words from a list under the appropriate category.

Note: If the final sound of the base word is voiced, -ed will make the sound /d/ (e.g., *mowed*, *planned*, *crunched*). If the final consonant in the base word is unvoiced, -ed will make the sound /t/ (e.g., *backed*, *sipped*, *rushed*). If the final consonant in the base word is /d/ or /t/, -ed will make the sound /ed/ (e.g., *tested*, *needed*, *landed*).

Talking Points for Professional Development:

▶ What's the difference between dividing a word into syllables based on phonology vs. dividing by morphology or orthography? Is there a moment where these different types of division could be clearer?

▶ To simplify this activity even more, could the teacher start with the base word and then add the -ed? Then, the student could listen for the final sound.

▶ How much additional practice is going to be necessary?

▶ Notice how the teacher always said something positive about the student's incorrect answer, then guided the student to the correct answer.

Multisyllabic Words

In this lesson, students are taught how to look for the vowel in a syllable, and how to divide words into syllables using syllable boards. Closed syllables with short vowels are used in this beginning lesson on longer words. (A closed syllable has one vowel followed by one or more consonants. Examples are: *at, Beth, if, bunch, jog*. The vowel is a closed syllable and usually has a short sound.)

Lesson Component:
Reading and spelling multisyllabic words.

Objective:
Students will read and spell two- and three-syllable words with short vowels.

Materials:
- White board or chart.
- Magnetized syllable boards; set of three for each student.
- Dry-erase markers and erasers.
- Paper and pencil for students.
- Word cards (*napkin, rabbit, kickback, hotdog, laptop, kitten, sunset, hilltop, bathtub, jetlag, bobcat, pigpen, basket, mitten, helmet, backpack, onset*). *Note:* These words all have closed syllables in short vowels ending in one or more consonants.

Instructional Procedure—Reading Multisyllabic Words:

- Write the word *napkin* on the board.
- Explain that each syllable has a vowel.
  - Say, *To read unfamiliar words, we look for the vowels, because every syllable has a vowel sound. If the vowels are apart, they belong in different syllables.*
  - Ask, *How many vowels do you see? Are they together or apart? Because they are apart, there are two syllables.*
- Put up two syllable boards; write *nap* on one and *kin* on the other.
- Explain that we usually break words between consonants: nap/kin. (The natural breaks in speaking a word are not the same as the conventions for breaking up words in print.)
- Try another word or two, with student help. Find the vowels, and write the syllables on syllable boards. Demonstrate that digraphs stay together: ath-let-ic; Munch-kin.

I DO

- Use words with all closed syllables for beginning syllable work.
- Give each student two word cards. Ask each student to:

  –Count the vowels.

  –Put one syllable board down for each syllable.

  –Write the syllables on syllable boards.

  –Read each syllable.

  –Blend the syllables into a word.

- Ensure that students know the meaning of the words they are reading.
- Examples of words with closed syllables: *imprint, fantastic, rabbit, comment, helmet, volcanic, magnetic.*

Instructional Procedure—Spelling Multisyllabic Words:

- Show students how to spell the words *cactus* and *catnip* by syllable:

  –Say each syllable.

  –Put one syllable board down for each syllable.

  –Write each syllable on a syllable board.

  –Write the word as a whole word on paper.

- Give students three words to spell (*penmanship, Atlantic, disinfect*); have them orally segment the syllables. Help them say the syllables, emphasizing the correct vowel sounds.
- Have students put one syllable board down for each syllable.
- Have students say and spell each syllable on the syllable boards.
- After students have spelled the syllables accurately on the syllable boards, have them turn the syllable boards over and spell the word on white boards.
- Have students turn the syllable boards over to check their spelling.
- Be sure the students know the meaning of the words they are spelling.
- Continue this strategy with students, reading and spelling more words.
- Ask students to use the words in a sentence.

Talking Points for Professional Development:

▶ Is it necessary to teach syllable division rules (VCCV, VCV) before students begin to break words up into syllables?

▶ Note how the teacher doesn't ask students to define words, but asks them to put the words in a sentence. Is this easier or more difficult than defining?

Understanding Schwa

Unaccented syllables are common in multisyllabic words. The vowel sound in those syllables is often a schwa. When students are given the name for this vowel sound, and practice identifying it, they can more readily "flex" while reading the vowels in unknown words. They can also understand that there is a reason why some vowels are not easily sounded out during spelling.

Lesson Component:
Reading and spelling multisyllable words.

Objective:
Students will identify and pronounce unaccented syllables (with schwa) in regular multisyllable words.

Materials:
- Magnetic syllable boards for teacher.
- Letter tile with schwa symbol ə.
- Three syllable boards for students.
- Header cards with *a, e, i, o, u.*
- Cards with multisyllabic words that have closed syllables and one schwa (e.g., *wagon, canal, ribbon*). (Do not underline the schwa on the word cards.)
- Transparent chips for students to place over schwa syllables on word cards.

Instructional Procedure:

I DO

- Say, *astonish* naturally, with an unaccented first syllable. Explain to students that many vowels in longer words have an indistinct sound when they are spoken, like the /uh/ in *astonish, about,* and *around*. We call this a schwa.
- Schwa, the lazy vowel sound, happens in syllables that are not stressed. We can identify the stressed and unstressed syllables by pretending to call a dog named "astonish." Tell students that the stressed syllable is the one you dwell on the longest (*ton* in *astonished*). The other syllables are unstressed.
- Show students a word card with the word *astonish* on it. Break the word into syllables on syllable boards: *a ston ish.*
- Schwa often sounds like a short *u*, as with the first syllable in *astonish*. But sometimes it can sound like a short *i*, as in *attic.*
- Show students the letter tile with the dictionary symbol for the schwa (ə) and place it over *a* on the first syllable board.

I DO
- Tell students that the schwa sound can be represented by any vowel letter.
- Place *a, e, i, o, u* on the table or in a pocket chart.
- Show the students the word *astonish.* Tell them the letter *a* spells the schwa sound, so you will put it under the *a.*

WE DO
- Hold up the word card for *recommend.* Ask a student to read the word.
- Ask a student to pretend to call a dog named "recommend." Remind students that the stressed syllable is the one you dwell on the longest (*mend*). Because the schwa appears in unstressed syllables only, it must be in one of the other syllables in *recommend.*
- Ask students to figure out which vowel is a schwa. It's the one that does not have the expected sound that matches the spelling. (In the first and final syllables the short *e* is heard, so the schwa must be in the middle syllable. The *o* in the middle syllable sounds like /uh/, which is a schwa sound.)

YOU DO
- Give each student one or more cards with multisyllabic words. Have students determine which letter represents a schwa sound. Students put a transparent marker over the vowel letter that represents schwa. After you check the student's answer, have the student remove the marker and put the card under the header letter in the word that represents the schwa.
- Ask individual students to explain what we mean by "schwa" (an indistinct or lazy vowel) and in what kind of syllable we find it (unaccented).

Scaffolding:
- If students are having trouble hearing the unaccented syllable, pull out syllable boards and work through the pronunciation of each syllable.
- Understanding schwa is more important for spelling than reading. However, exposure to the concept facilitates reading multisyllabic words in a "natural" way. Model "natural" vs. "contrived" pronunciation to help students remember spelling. (Contrived pronunciation means that the short vowel sound is pronounced instead of the schwa.)

Talking Points for Professional Development:
▸ The reinforcement of using "flexing" is a brief point. However, note that the teacher continues to use that terminology after his brief introduction.
▸ How does vocabulary instruction get integrated into this "phonics" lesson?
▸ Notice how comfortable students are with short vowel letter sounds. This is necessary in order for students to read multisyllabic words with accuracy and fluency.
▸ Why is it important to teach students about schwa?

Teaching Magic *e*

VC*e* is the most predictable long vowel spelling type. Note that the pattern works when the syllable has a long vowel spelled with one vowel letter, and one consonant between the long vowel and final silent *e*. Here the pattern is taught to second graders.

Lesson Component:
Advanced decoding, long vowels.

Objective:
Students will know that a vowel plus a consonant followed by an *e* spells the long vowel phoneme.

Materials:
- Small letter tiles to spell *mad, pet, hid, hop, cut*, and five *e* letter tiles to spell *made, Pete, hide, hope, cute*.
- White board for teacher
- White boards for students
- Pencils
- Dry-erase markers and erasers
- Timers or stopwatches
- Teacher lists:
  – Guide words for introducing VC*e* spellings for each long vowel sound
  – Spelling dictation
- Word cards
- Worksheets for each student:
  – Guide word chart
  – Fluency builder worksheet
  – Spelling dictation page

Instructional Procedure—Introducing the Concept of Silent e:
- Arrange letter tiles in "work space" set up as follows:

	a	b	c	d	e	f	
	g	h	i	j	k	l	
m	n	o	p	q	r	s	
t	u	v	w	x	y	z	
ch	sh	th	wh	ph	ck		

- Say, *Letters can represent more than one sound. Sometimes patterns of letters represent a sound.*
- Separate out vowel letter tiles (*a, e, i, o, u*). Review the known short vowel sounds.
- Say, *Sometimes a vowel letter will represent its own name. When it does, we call that the "long vowel sound."* Point to each vowel letter and have students produce the long vowel sound by saying the letter name.
- Explain that the letter *e* has many jobs. Say, *Sometimes e is called "magic e" or "bossy e" because it can make another vowel say its own name. An **e** after one consonant that follows one vowel works with the vowel before the consonant by reaching back over the single consonant and making the first vowel say its own name.*
- Using the teacher letter tiles, put *mad* on the board. Ask students to sound out the word.
- Place the *e* letter tile at the end, making *made*. Explain to students that the *e* works with the *a* to help the *a* say its own name, the long vowel sound. Draw an arrow from the *e* back over the *d* to the *a*.
- Touch and say this pattern by touching the *a* and *e* at the same time (using two fingers) as you say the long *a* sound, the touch the *t* and say /t/.
- Have students touch and say the sounds in the word, using two fingers to touch the *a* and *e* as they say the long *a* sound.
- Follow this pattern with the remaining words on the letter tile word list: *pet, hid, hop, cut* changed to *pete, hide, hope, cute.*

Instructional Procedure—Making a Guide Word Chart:
- After all the silent *e* spellings have been introduced and all the silent *e* words are on the white board, explain that these are guide words for the long vowel spellings using silent *e*.
- Students study and take a mental picture of the guide words.
- Cover the white board with the guide words on it.
- Students write the guide words on their white boards, then underline the vowel and the *e* and connect the two lines in each word while saying the long vowel sound.

- Uncover guide words on the whiteboard and have students check their work.
- Have students fill in a guide word chart, as in the following example:

Guide Word Chart
Silent *e* Spellings

Spelling	Guide Word
a-e	m<u>ade</u>
e – e	P<u>ete</u>
i – e	h<u>ide</u>
o – e	h<u>ope</u>
u - e	c<u>ube</u>

Instructional Procedure—Practicing Silent e With White Board Writing:

- Review the pattern for silent *e*.
- Hand out white boards and markers.
- Have students write the word *not* on their boards.
- Touch and say the word together.
- Ask students to add the magic *e* to the end, then touch and say together again for the new word, *note*.
- Practice this pattern with the remaining words, gradually leaving off touch and say (*grim / grime, slop/slope, glob/globe, tap/tape, rat/rate, van/vane, hat/hate, at/ate, shin/shin, cut/cute, scrap/scrape, slid/slide, quit/quite, plan/plane*).

Instructional Procedure—Practicing Silent e With Word Sort:

- Review the pattern for silent *e*.
- Hand out several word cards to each student.
- Ask students to read the word on a card and determine whether it fits the VC*e* pattern. (If a student is having difficulty figuring out the word, ask him or her to touch and say the word. Use this strategy as a "fall back," because students should move beyond the need to use this strategy.)
- Sort the cards into two piles (those that have a long vowel sound, and those that have a short vowel sound.)
- Examples of words on cards: *pet, Pete, cut, cute, them, theme, rid, ride, quit, quite, slid, slide, hop, hope, rob, robe, glob, globe, cub, cube, at, ate, slim, slime, slop, slope, plan, plane, scrap, scrape, shin, shine, plan, plane, cut, cute.*

Instructional Procedure—Practicing Silent e by Marking the Word List:

- Review the pattern for silent *e*.

- Hand out printed word lists, with VC*e* and words with closed syllables, and pencils.

- Ask students to read each word and underline the letters that spell the vowel sound, connecting the vowel and the *e* in silent *e* words. For example, for the word *jive*, students would underline the letters *i* and *e* and connect those letters with a line. For the word *stand*, students would underline the letter *a*. Students read each word aloud and circle words that follow the VC*e* pattern.

- Guide students through marking the first two or three words.

- When students understand the pattern, have them finish the sheet on their own.

- When they are finished, read the words together.

Instructional Procedure—Practicing Silent e With Speed Drill Word List:

- Review the pattern for silent *e*.

- Divide students into teams of three.

- Hand out speed drill word lists and timers or stopwatches.

- Have students chorally read the word lists to make sure they know all the words. Do not practice timed readings until everyone has read the words.

- When they are comfortable with all the words, they are ready for the fluency drill. With partners, students time each other to see how quickly each student can read the list. One student times, one student reads, and one student checks for accuracy.

- Have students trade roles.

Spelling and Dictation:

- Dictate words that have both short vowels and long vowels spelled with magic *e*. Also dictate sentences with both magic *e* and short vowel words.

  –Real words: *shade, spit, mile, hope, glad, cube, rot, bud.*

  –Sentences: "Pete pets the tame cub." "It is not quite time to quit."

- Have students write words or sentences.

- Show the correct spelling so students can check their answers.

Talking Points for Professional Development:

▸ Note how the teacher introduces the topic to students.

▸ A few kindergarten phonological awareness programs emphasize having students identify the vowel sound in a spoken word and state whether the vowel is long or short. How would this early instruction help students with this lesson?

▸ What difficulty might be expected after this lesson if students don't know the difference between long and short vowel sounds?

▸ How could the teacher make sure students know the difference between long and short vowel sounds before beginning the intruction about silent *e*?

Multisyllabic Words With Magic e

The vowel-consonant-*e* pattern, or VC*e*, is the syllable type most readily combined with closed or short vowel syllables as students are learning to read longer words. VC*e* in longer words is often found at the end. Some VC*e* final syllables are odd; they are pronounced with schwa or an indistinct vowel. They should be avoided in the first few lessons or until students understand schwa (e.g., *elective, cornice*).

Lesson Component:

Reading and spelling multisyllabic words.

Objective:

Students will read and spell two- and three-syllable words with short vowel and silent *e* syllables.

Materials:

- Syllable boards with magnets for teacher
- Sets of four syllable boards for students
- Dry-erase markers and erasers
- Paper and pencil for students
- Word Cards, closed and Magic *e* syllable combinations

Instructional Procedure:

- Remind students that they can read multisyllable words with short vowels by counting the vowels, noticing if they are together or apart, then breaking the word into syllables, with a vowel in each syllable. Demonstrate with *establish*.

- Say, *Now that you know how to read magic **e** words, you can read words with more than one syllable if one of the syllables has a magic **e**. Just look for the magic **e** and make sure it stays in the syllable with another vowel.* Demonstrate with valentine, and say,

  I DO

  WE DO

  – *Let's look at this word,* **valentine.**

  – *How many vowels do you see?*

  – *Are they together or apart?*

  – *Do you see a magic **e**?*

  – *The **e** in a magic **e** syllable will stick with the other vowel in a syllable.*

  – *There are three syllables, one for the vowel **a**, one for the vowel **e**, and one for the vowels **i** and **e**. Write each syllable on a syllable board.*

  – *Who would like to read each syllable?*

  – *Who wants to read the word?*

YOU DO

- Give each student two word cards. Ask each student to count the vowels, notice if there is a silent *e*, break the words into syllables on syllable boards, read each syllable, and blend the syllables into words.

- Examples:

frustrate, incomplete	*escape, illustrate*	*include, demonstrate*
statement, substitute	*athlete, compensate*	

Talking Points for Professional Development:

▸ Is it important to clarify for the student the closed syllables or syllable division rules in words (e.g., *valentine*)?

▸ Note how many repetitions the teacher encourages for the word *magnetic*. Why does he spend so much time on this?

▸ The student breaks the word *valentine* with the first syllable as *va*. Notice that the teacher helped the student "flex" the sound from /uh/ to short *a* instead of changing the spelling of the syllable. This is because the first choice for breaking a multisyllabic word with the VCVC pattern is to break between the first vowel and the consonant. This method teaches children to use their best skills to break words into syllables, then flex the sounds, instead of moving letters from syllable to syllable.

Spellings for /er/

Vowel-*r* patterns (or "*r*-controlled") are difficult to spell because the vowel sound is not readily separable from /r/, especially with the /er/ sound, and there are multiple spellings for /er/, /r/, and /or/. In the lesson, the teacher introduces the most common spellings for /er/. Students often need a great deal of experience and practice to learn words with the /er/ sound because there are so many different spellings for just one sound.

Lesson Component:
Spelling complex vowel patterns.

Objective:
Students will learn guide words for the *ir*, *ur*, and *er* spellings of /er/.

Materials:
- Guide word charts for students to complete.
- Letter tiles to spell guide words *her*, *bird*, and *turn*; (h er, b ir d, t ur n)
- White boards and markers.

Instructional Procedure—Introducing the Spellings for /er/:
- Explain to students that they will learn three ways to spell the sound /er/.
- With letter tiles, spell the first guide word, *her*, on the white board (h er).
- Underline the letter combination that spells /er/ (er).
- Have each student touches and says the sounds in the word, blending them together.
- Repeat for each guide word: *bird* (b ir d) and *turn* (t ur n).

Instructional Procedure—Learning the Spellings and Filling in the Guide Word Chart:
- Leave the words *her*, *bird*, and *turn* on the white board, and explain that these are guide words for the three /er/ spellings students learned today.
- Have students study and take a mental picture of the guide words.
- Cover the white board with the guide words on it.
- Have students write the guide words on their white boards and underline the letters that spell /er/ in each word.
- Uncover the guide words on the white board and have students check their work.
- Have students fill in the guide word chart.

- Explain that the guide word chart has three additional slots for three more spellings to be learned in another lesson.

Guide Word Chart
/er/ Spellings

Spelling	Guide Word
er	h<u>er</u>
ir	b<u>ir</u>d
ur	t<u>ur</u>n

Note: Follow-up activities include sorting words by spelling pattern, reading phrases, sentences, and text with vowel-*r* words, spelling words, and writing sentences to dictation.

Talking Points for Professional Development:

▶ Vowel-*r* combinations /er/, /ar/, and /or/ are different phonologically. How are /ar/ and /or/ different from /er/? Why do kids spell *brid* instead of *bird*?

▶ What kind of phonological awareness exercises could be a good warm up for this lesson?

Fluency: Long o

To introduce long *o*, the teacher explicitly teaches the possible spellings and a guide word for each spelling. The guide words help students remember the spellings. The less common "ough" spelling for long *o* (as in *though*) is not taught in this introductory lesson for third graders.

Note: Only part of the lesson is shown here because of its length.

Lesson Component:
Decoding and spelling complex vowel patterns.

Objective:
Students will read and write guide words that spell the long *o* sound: *o*, *ow*, *oe*, *oa*, and *o-e*.

Materials:
- Large letter tiles for introducing *o*, *oa*, *o-e*, *ow*, and *oe*.
- Large letter tiles to spell guide words *go*, *boat*, *note*, *snow*, and *toe*.
- Student white boards.
- Dry-erase markers and erasers.
- Pencils.
- Word cards for sorting.
- Worksheet packet for each student:
  - Guide word chart
  - Fluency word list
  - Sentences
  - Spelling grid
  - Decodable story

Instructional Procedure—Introducing Long o Spellings:
- Announce the phoneme of the day, /ō/. Have students repeat the sound /ō/. Explain that we are going to learn five common ways to spell the sound /ō/.
- Spell the first guide word, *go*, with letter tiles. Touch and say the sounds in *go*. Ask students what the spelling for the sound long *o* is. Underline the letter *o*.

- Continue with each word, underlining the spelling for /ō/ and adding the letter tile for the spelling to the right of the word. Continue for the remaining four common spellings:

oa, boat
oe, toe
ow, snow
o-e, note

Instructional Procedure—Learning the Spellings and Filling in the Guide Word Chart:

- Leave the guide words on the white board, and explain that these are guide words for the long *o* spellings students learned today.
- Have students study and take a mental picture of the guide words.
- Cover the white board with the guide words on it.
- Have students write the guide words on their white boards and underline the letters that spell long *o* in each word.
- Uncover the guide words on the white board, and have students check their work.
- Have students fill in the guide word chart.
- Explain that there is a sixth space for a less common spelling.

Guide Word Chart
Long *o* Spellings

Spelling	Guide Word
o	g<u>o</u>
oa	b<u>oa</u>t
o – e	n<u>ote</u>
ow	sn<u>ow</u>
oe	t<u>oe</u>

Extension Activity: Sort Word Cards for Five Spellings:

- Prepare a deck of cards with the long vowel spellings. Words on cards might include:
  - Flash words, high frequency words, spelled with long o phonics patterns, that we need to know how to read and spell "in a flash": *no, over, old, so, know, also, cold, own, open, show,* and *those.*
  - Decodable words: *home, road, rode, hole, whole, hoe, goes, yellow, follow, soap, toast, coast, throat, float,* and *bowl.*

- Ask students to name the five spellings. Place the large letter tiles on the table as each spelling is named.
- Students take turns drawing a card, reading the word, saying the letters that spell /ō/, and then placing the card under the appropriate letter tile.

Spelling and Dictation:

Dictate some of the words from the word card deck used for the sorting activity. Have students write the spellings of *o* across the top of a piece of paper. Students spell the words in the appropriate columns for the /ō/ spelling, as in the following chart.

o	oa	oe	ow	o-e
over	road	hoe	own	home
old	soap	goes	show	rode
so	coast	tiptoe	yellow	whole
also	toast		follow	hole
cold	throat		bowl	
open	float		window	

Talking Points for Professional Development:

▸ In word sorting, what would you keep in mind to select the words to sort?

▸ At what moments are students' vocabulary issues visible?

▸ How could the teacher include homophones (*whole, hole*) as part of the lesson?

▸ Discuss the reasons for presenting all the spellings for one sound as opposed to introducing a spelling and presenting all the sounds (e.g., *ea* can spell /ē/ as in *bead*, /ĕ/ as in *bread*, and /ā/ as in *great*.)

Part 5: Teaching Vocabulary and Comprehension

Who is vocabulary and comprehension instruction for?

Vocabulary and comprehension should be taught at all levels of reading ability, starting even before students attend school. Instruction in word meanings, word structure, word relationships, and text comprehension is appropriate in any grade. When students do not read well, vocabulary and comprehension can be taught when teachers read aloud. All the components of good reading instruction, including phonological awareness, phonics, fluency, vocabulary, comprehension, spelling, and writing, are best taught in parallel.

Why use these teaching techniques?

Many novice readers need help learning how to navigate and understand a text. They benefit from direct teaching about text structure, word meanings, and productive strategies for text comprehension. They should be pressed to think hard, to question during reading, to make connections between sources of information, and to expect that they will be able to comprehend if they are persistent. Eventually, the "strategies" they learn must become a habit of thought, not a self-conscious process.

How are vocabulary and comprehension best taught?

Many volumes have been written about vocabulary and comprehension instruction in reading. Throughout *Teaching Reading Essentials*, we aim to show that vocabulary development can be an aspect of phonological and phonics instruction, as well as a contributor to reading fluency. Some words that students need to know can be directly taught. Other words will be learned during reading itself and from incidental teaching of word meanings. The best ways for students to learn word meanings are to read and to increase their knowledge of the world. The job of the teacher is to help the student construct the meanings intended by the author of the text. In these demonstrations, the teachers use a variety of techniques proven by research to be effective, including:

- Asking students to make a mental picture as they read.
- Asking questions during reading; predicting what might happen next.

- Summarizing and retelling parts or all of a text.
- Drawing connections between the information in the text and students' experiences.
- Using graphic organizers to depict conceptual relationships.

DVD Navigation

Part 5: Teaching Vocabulary and Comprehension			
For all students			
Demonstration Video	**Activity Name**	**Page**	**Time (minutes)**
	Introduction to Part 5	123	12:29
Word Meaning Activities			
1	Categorizing Words	125	8:25
2	Multiple Meanings	127	30:05
3	Scaling Words	130	2:26
4	Introducing Morphemes Professional Development Session	132	14:24 6:17
Integrated Lessons			
5	Comprehension Strategies Professional Development Session	134	16:05 21:08
6	Supported Writing	136	13:47

Categorizing Words

Categorizing words helps students make connections between words; think about similarities and differences between words, and think about reasons for choices. When students categorize words, they are developing skills that will help them organize their ideas as they write. Categorizing activities are beneficial in kindergarten (sort animals by whether they fly or walk) through high school (sort words by their language of origin).

Lesson Component:

Vocabulary.

Objective:

Students will categorize words related to a text reading and explain the reasons for word groupings.

Materials:

- Words on index cards for categorizing. (Words should be connected to topic or theme being studied or read about.)
- Graphic organizer showing the main, unifying category and subcategories with boxes underneath subcategories.

Instructional Procedure:

- Select words from a recent reading and write each word on an index card.
- Put word cards out on the table or on the board.
- Read the cards together as a class.
- Ask students what story they just read.
- Write the name of the story on an index card and tell the students that all the words they read came from that story.
- Put the card with the name of the story as the main, unifying category.
- Suggest words describing three or four basic categories that the words can be grouped within. Make header cards for those words and place them under the name of the story.
- Ask students to read each card and place the cards into the appropriate category.

Alternate Procedure—Discover the Categories:

- Give each pair or group of students a set of word cards.

- Have them group the words and decide what the categories should be.

- Have the group make category cards as they sort the words into related groups, then have them put the cards under the appropriate category card.

- Have students check the words and the accuracy of their category headings.

- Ask if there are any other ways the words might be grouped or defined. If so, move them around accordingly and re-title the groups.

Alternate Procedure—Using a Graphic Organizer:

- Hand out a blank graphic organizer, as pictured below, with a list of words that includes the word for the main category and the words for the subcategories.

- Ask students to categorize the words using the graphic organizer.

- When everyone has finished, go over the ideas that students have come up with for categories and subcategories, and discuss and how they sorted the words. Allow categories that make sense and that can be defended by the person doing the grouping.

Note: This activity is much easier if the categories are written on the graphic organizer and only words that are to be sorted are included in the word list.

Words to categorize would be listed here.

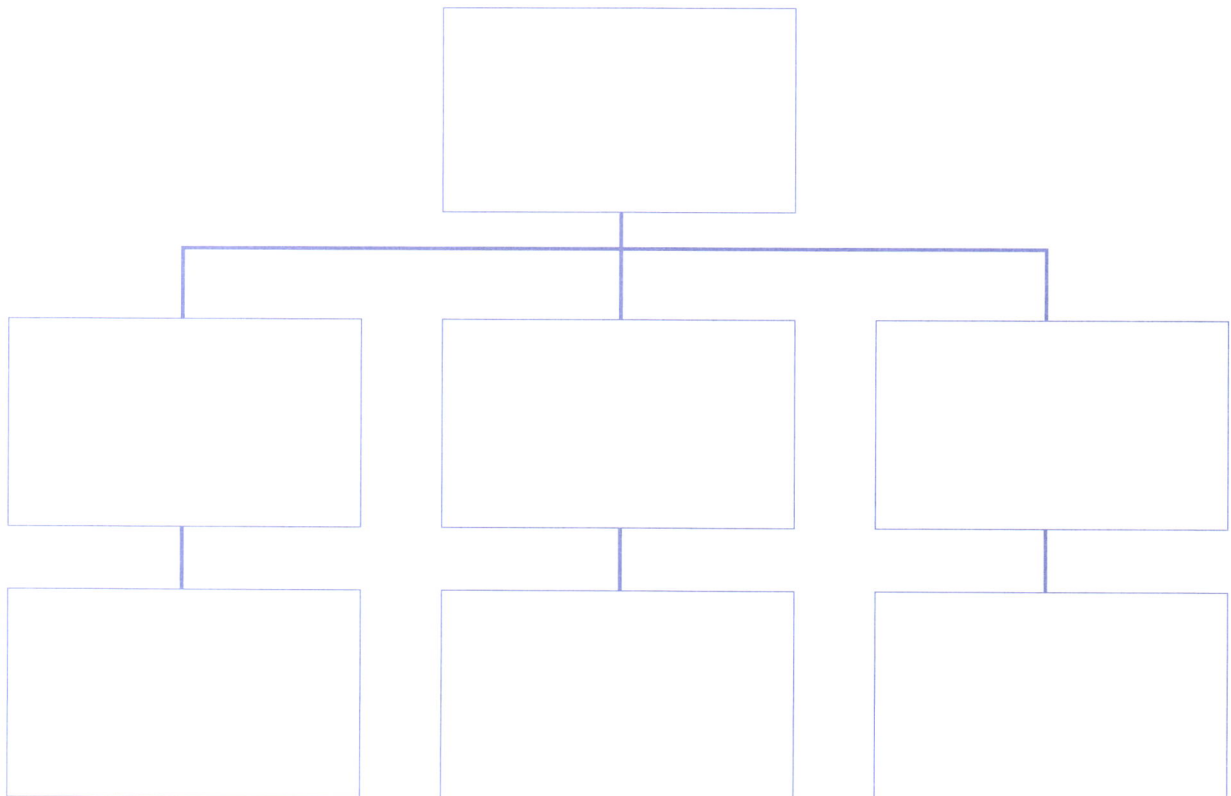

Multiple Meanings

In this demonstration, the teacher draws on text from *Amelia Bedelia* to teach a group of third-grade students that words can have multiple meanings.

Lesson Component:
Vocabulary.

Objective:
Students will anticipate, recognize, and use alternate meanings of common words.

Materials:
- List of common words with multiple meanings.
- Multiple meaning organizer for each student.
- White board or chalkboard.

Instructional Procedure:
Prepare for Lesson
- Select a section of a book with several words that have multiple meanings.
- Read a section of a book or have students read the selection. (An alternative is to select words from a book the students have recently read.)

I DO
- Tell students that common words often have more than one meaning and use. For example, the word *run* has many meanings the students already know.
- Tell students two meanings you know for the word.
- Pass out a multiple meaning organizer to each student.
- Demonstrate using the organizer by filling in the word *run* and your meanings, with a brief definition and a sentence for each meaning.

WE DO
- Have students fill in their word webs with the word *run* and your two meanings.
- Brainstorm with students for two or three additional known meanings for *run*.
- Demonstrate the completion of the multiple meaning organizer for the word *run*. (The organizer contains space for the word, a brief definition of each meaning, and a sentence based on each meaning.)
- Select another multiple meaning word from the passage.
- Have students put the word at the top of the organizer.
- Discuss the multiple meanings for the word.
- Help students complete the organizer.

YOU DO

- Select another word or words from the passage. Read the sentence in which that word is embedded.
- Discuss meanings of the word.
- Have students fill in the organizer.
- If appropriate, direct students to the dictionary for additional meanings or clarification.

Multiple Meaning Organizer

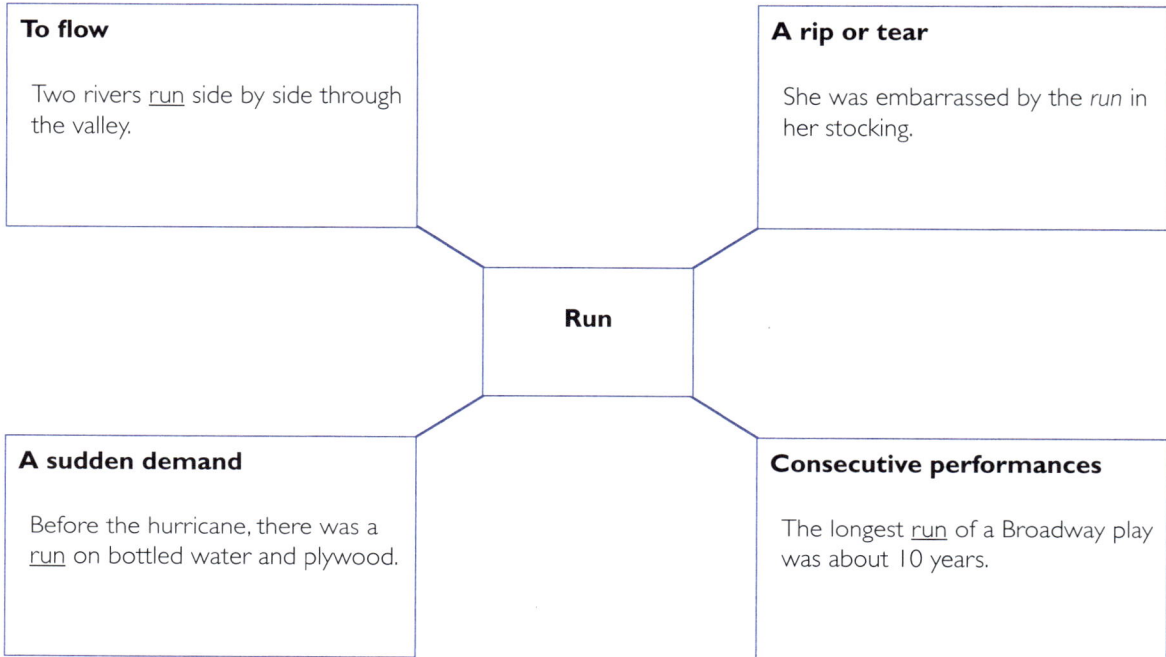

To flow	**A rip or tear**
Two rivers <u>run</u> side by side through the valley.	She was embarrassed by the *run* in her stocking.

Run

A sudden demand	**Consecutive performances**
Before the hurricane, there was a <u>run</u> on bottled water and plywood.	The longest <u>run</u> of a Broadway play was about 10 years.

Multiple Meaning Organizer

Word: _____ Run.

1. Definition: _____ To flow.
   Sentence: _____ Two rivers run side by side through the valley.

   _____

2. Definition: _____ A rip or tear.
   Sentence: _____ She was embarrased by the run in her stocking.

   _____

3. Definition: <u>A sudden demand.</u>

   Sentence: <u>Before the hurricane, there was a run on bottled water and plywood.</u>

4. Definition: <u>Consecutive performances.</u>

   Sentence: <u>The longest run of a Broadway play was about 10 years.</u>

5. Definition: _____

   Sentence: _____

   _____

Talking Points for Professional Development:

▸ The teacher connects book reading to this activity, extending language play. Why base the activity on *Amelia Bedelia*?

▸ The teacher changes a student's non-standard sentence to a standard sentence for writing. How and why?

▸ Why should the students use the words orally in well constructed sentences?

▸ The graphic organizer works for the teacher because it is enlarged, but students might have trouble writing in a smaller version. The second organizer above might be easier for writing.

Scaling Words

This activity, appropriate for developing greater precision in word use and word interpretation, is focused on descriptive terms that represent a continuum of meaning along an attribute scale.

Lesson Component:
Vocabulary.

Objective:
Students will demonstrate understanding of gradations of meaning in a set of related terms.

Materials:
- White board/chalkboard with an image of a balance scale:
- Word card sets for scalable attributes such as: (words to begin the activity are underlined)

    –*hideous, ugly, homely, fair, pretty beautiful, stunning, gorgeous*
    –*microscopic, miniscule, tiny, small, large, huge, gigantic, monstrous*
    –*grief-stricken, morose, depressed, sad, glad, happy, delighted, overjoyed, ecstatic.*

- Other antonyms, such as *hot/cold, high/low.*

Instructional Procedures:
Demonstrate Activity

- Show students a gradable antonym pair, such as *hot/cold.* Ask if they think of these words as opposites (antonyms).
- Then ask, *So what would we do with the word, **warm**? Does it fit between the opposites?* (Yes.)
- Show the idea of a meaning scale by putting word cards for *hot* and *cold* on opposite ends of the scale. Point out that opposites sit on either side of the balance point.
- Explain that even though some words are opposites on the meaning scale, many words can fit in between the words and that some words can fit beyond those words, farther out on the scale.
- Using words that describe temperature (e.g., *tepid, frigid, scalding, boiling*), work through a scaling exercise together as a class.
- Pick another set of opposite terms and work through another scaling exercise as a group. Discuss the possibility that people might have different interpretations on the ordering of some terms; for example, one student might place *attractive* beyond *pretty* while another might place it closer to the center on the meaning scale.

Students Work in Groups

- Group students into small groups.

- Give each group a set of cards that will fit in a scaled set.

- Ask each group to arrange the terms and then think of objects, people, animals, or ideas for which they would use each descriptive term.

- The dictionary can be consulted, as definition entries often list synonyms and antonyms for words. A thesaurus is also a good resource for this activity.

- Once all groups have finished organizing their words, ask each group to share their word set with the class.

Talking Points for Professional Development:

▸ What kind of words are best suited for this activity?

▸ After a scaling activity, what kind of follow-up might be necessary to get children to apply what they've learned?

Introducing Morphemes

Morphemes are the smallest meaningful unit of language. Morphemes may be whole words but are often parts of words that combine with others to make words. Content words in English are often derived from Latin or Greek. English words derived from Latin have roots that combine with prefixes and suffixes. English words derived from Greek often have two roots. The third graders in this demonstration are introduced to the idea of a meaningful part of a word, *spect*, meaning "see" in Latin.

Lesson Component:
Vocabulary.

Objective:
Students will learn the meaning of a new word by relating it to to a known word that shares a root morpheme.

Materials:
- Word already taught or known by students or words from a current text reading or topic of study.
- A family of words morphologically related to the known word.
- White board or chalkboard.

Instructional Procedure:
- Refer to the text in which the word was used.
- Write the known word and a new word on the board.
- Ask students to compare the two words and find the parts that are similar.
- Discuss possible meanings of the new vocabulary word in light of the word or words in that family that are already known.
- Read the passage.
- Discuss the meaning of the new word again to see if students have any additional thoughts about it.
- Ask students for any personal connection with the new word.
- Have students compose two sentences, one for the known word and one that uses the new word.
- Examples of known/new words: *migrate/immigrant*; *family/familiar*; *inspect/spectacle/ prospector*.

Talking Points for Professional Development:

▸ Students confuse similar sounding words (*inspect/expect*); why would such confusions occur?

▸ How does the teacher use new words frequently and encourage students to do the same?

▸ How is the lesson concluded?

▸ This demonstration shows an incidental or context-related opportunity for instruction. How might a systematic, explicit program of instruction in morphology be organized?

Comprehension Strategies

The focus of this lesson is story structure. These third grade students learn that every story has a problem and a solution to that problem. Supported reading strategies include previewing the text, asking questions to clarify meanings, and summarizing. The teacher tells the students explicitly to locate and label the problem in the story and the solution that unfolds.

Lesson Component:
Comprehension.

Objective:
Students will read and understand level-appropriate connected text.

Materials:
Level-appropriate books.

Instructional Procedures:
- Provide a reading passage containing sound-symbol patterns and words that have been taught. The student should not miss more than one word in five, or the book is too difficult.
- Briefly point out the title, topic, and first few illustrations, and discuss what the story might be about. From this preview should come a stated purpose for reading (e.g., understanding the story's problem and its solution).
- Pre-teach any vocabulary essential for understanding the text. Ask students to browse the passage to see if there are words they may find difficult. Provide assistance with either decoding or meaning for those words.
- Ask students to make predictions about the book, such as what might happen, what the book is about, and why they think so. Return to those predictions after reading and check to see if they were right.
- Questions that elicit good responses from children before, during, and after reading often focus on the following thought processes:
  - Understanding a sequence of events.
  - Understanding cause and effect—the *why* of the story or informational piece.
  - Clarification of a point, event or word meaning that is obscure or that could be misunderstood.
  - Stating a main idea or set of main ideas.
  - Understanding the logical structure or narrative structure of the text.
  - Visualizing and describing what is taking place.

- Questioning should focus on the aspects of a particular text that are of most interest or relevance to students or should be oriented toward the intended purpose for reading. Narrative texts, or stories, will be appropriate for questions about setting, character, and plot. Expository or factual texts will be appropriate for questions about cause and effect relationships or the organization of the natural world. A *query*, or probing question, will often require more than a simple, text-based response.

- Examples of good questions:

  Why do you think that happened?

  Why would the author tell us that here?

  Does this remind you of something that happened earlier in the story?

  Is the author holding information back? Why?

  What do we know about this character so far?

  Does this place remind you of any you have been before?

  Do you like the way this story ended? Why or why or why not?

Talking Points for Professional Development:

▸ What pre-reading activities are used before reading? Why?

▸ What does the teacher do during reading? How many strategies can you identify?

▸ What does the teacher do after reading?

Supported Writing

Written responses to reading require students to engage in deeper, more thoughtful processing of text meanings.

Lesson Component:
Comprehension and composition.

Objective:
After reading a book or passage, students will develop their thoughts about the story using oral language, and compose a sentence, group of sentences, or organized paragraph in response to what they read.

Materials:
- Level-appropriate books.
- Chart or white board.
- Paper and pencil, or student journals.

Instructional Procedures:
- **Beginner:** After students have read and reread a book, ask one student to orally formulate a sentence about the story that the other students can then recite. Help all students write the sentence, reminding them to use the spellings, letter formation, and punctuation skills they have learned. Consult high-frequency word lists, personal spelling dictionaries, and other guides to increase student self-reliance.

- **More advanced:** Ask each student to write his or her response to a question that you or a student has raised about the book. For example, *How did (character) solve her problem?* or *How did you feel about (character)? Why?* or *What would you have done if you had been (character)?*

- Encourage students to read their work orally to themselves or to one another, then correct their work. Check students' papers and give feedback. Do not leave errors uncorrected when you check papers if they involve a skill that has been taught.

- Re-teach any component skills that students did not understand in this lesson.

Talking Points for Professional Development:

▸ What correction strategy is used when the student misspells *found*?

▸ Why would the student want to spell the word *tangled* t-a-ng-g-el-d?

▸ How does the teacher provide structure and scaffolding?

Appendices

Appendix A: Research Base for *Teaching Reading Essentials*

Purpose

Over the past two decades, a solid consensus on the components of effective reading instruction has been reached (e.g., National Institute of Child Health and Human Development (NICHD), 2000a). Even so, the process of translating this knowledge into teacher practice has been relatively slow. The good news is that more school districts are pursuing professional development that emphasizes conceptually sound and empirically valid instructional methods in reading. However, many teachers are unable to apply even well-designed professional development without assistance in the form of coaching, mentoring, or follow-up instruction (Anders, Hoffman, & Duffy, 2000).

The gap between the knowledge base cultivated in workshops and institutes and teachers' classroom practices receives little attention because follow-up mentoring is logistically difficult and costly. Another problem is that the success of follow-up mentoring depends on the knowledge and skill of the mentor or coach. *Teaching Reading Essentials* addresses the gap that exists between teacher training and effective classroom and small-group practice by providing educators with 58 video lesson demonstrations of effective strategies for reading instruction. The lessons are authentic beginning reading instruction with small groups of children. All of the video demonstrations show real teachers and real students who have not rehearsed any part of the lessons.

The *Teaching Reading Essentials* lessons use linguistically informed, structured, explicit, sequential, engaging, and mulitsensory techniques that are appropriate for remediation of reading problems and for classroom reading instruction. Most importantly, the lesson demonstrations are based on hundreds of reading research studies that report a strong consensus on how children learn to read, why many children fail to learn adequately, and what components and methods in reading instruction are likely to be effective.

The lesson presentations are designed to illustrate the specific strategies that teachers need to learn and implement and will learn best through watching effective modeling and demonstration. *Teaching Reading Essentials* shows teachers how, *during instruction,* they must

- differentiate between phonemes (sounds) and graphemes (letters and letter combinations that represent sounds)
- call attention to the articulatory features of speech sounds
- use multisensory sound blending techniques
- teach orthographic patterns
- guide students into a decoding habit
- use memory strategies for irregular words
- follow reading with writing
- explore word meanings even while decoding skill is being established

- integrate vocabulary and comprehension strategies into decoding lessons, and integrate decoding strategies into vocabulary and comprehension lessons

Teaching Reading Essentials videos also highlight, provide, and model

- the elements of spoken and written language that are likely to be challenging for novice readers

- a progression of word study instruction from simple letter-sound correspondences through syllable patterns and basic morphology

- a pace appropriate for novice readers

- clear, explicit definitions of concepts

- active engagement in exploration of orthographic patterns

- systematic building of one concept about orthography on another

- a "model, lead, and apply" sequence throughout the lessons.

The lessons demonstrated in *Teaching Reading Essentials* complement any comprehensive, core reading instruction program that incorporates scientifically researched methods throughout. The program provides skill-building for teachers that is more explicit, detailed, and linguistically informed than publisher-funded, program-specific professional development.

Effective Integration

The accumulated evidence from two decades of educational and medical research supported by the National Institutes of Health (NIH) and the U.S. Department of Education shows that most reading problems are preventable (Lyon, 1998; Torgesen et al, 2001). Almost all children can learn to read if given excellent instruction at an early age. When appropriate instruction is delivered in kindergarten and first grade, and intensive help is provided for poor readers by third grade, the number of students who read below grade level can be reduced to anywhere from 2% to 6% (Torgesen, 2000).

Phonological Awareness and Phonics

Both the National Reading Panel and the Committee on the Prevention of Reading Difficulties agree that effective instruction consists of several components including systematic, direct teaching of phonological skill and phonics. Current educational policies at the federal, state, and district levels increasingly support the direct, systematic teaching of phoneme awareness and phonics to beginning readers and to students with reading and spelling difficulties.

A large body of research has demonstrated that the inability to process the phonological features of language and associate them with graphemes rapidly and accurately leads to weaknesses in word recognition, and undermines fluent reading and comprehension in childhood and adolescence (e.g., Torgesen et al., 2001). About 90% of all children who have reading difficulties show prominent and enduring problems with phonological skills (Shankweiler et al., 1999). Consistent phonemic instruction has produced gains in young readers (Torgesen, 2000), making poor readers good, and good readers better (Share & Stanovich, 1995; Francis et al., 1996).

Phoneme awareness and phonics instruction requires that the teacher have specific linguistic knowledge, skills, and the ability to carry out instructional routines. For example, phoneme awareness instruction requires the teacher to count, produce, blend, segment, and manipulate the individual speech sounds in words and to avoid confusing them with letters. Phonics instruction requires the teacher to lead students through multi-layered, complex, and variable spelling correspondences at the sound, syllable, and morpheme levels. Teachers of early reading must help students mentally represent and analyze the speech sounds within words because explicit awareness of sounds is necessary before exposure to print can increase knowledge of grapheme-phoneme correspondence (Moats & Foorman, 2003).

Teacher Level Variables Impact on Student Achievement

The results from several studies show that teachers' understanding of phonology and early reading instruction and their instructional practices affect student outcomes (e.g., McCutchen & Berninger, 1999; McCutchen et al., 2002; O'Conner, 1999). These findings are critically important in light of results from a recent NICHD-funded study (Foorman & Moats, 2004) showing that the majority of early elementary teachers working in high poverty urban schools in two major cities typically understood too little about spoken and written language structure to be able to teach reading and spelling explicitly and systematically. These results are consistent with previous findings that both inexperienced and experienced teachers: (a) have a weak grasp of phonological concepts and phonics (Moats, 1994, 1995; Moats & Lyon, 1996; Rath, 1994), (b) feel only somewhat prepared to teach struggling readers (Bos et al., 2001; Hill, 2000), and (c) lack knowledge of validated principles and supervised experience needed to address the needs of struggling readers (Lyon, Vaasen, & Toomey, 1989).

Failure to Translate Professional Development to Effective Teaching

Continuing professional development that teaches effective methods of instruction for teachers is a key ingredient in improving reading outcomes and preventing reading difficulties in students across all grades (Foorman and Moats, 2004; Moats and Foorman, 2003; Moats, 2004). Snow, Griffin, & Burns (2006) argue that in-service professional development should strengthen teaching skills, increase teacher knowledge of the reading process, and facilitate the integration of new research findings into the teaching practices of the classroom teacher. Despite the fact that in-service professional development has been shown to increase student achievement, on average teachers typically spend very little time extending their knowledge and skills base. The National Staff Development Council survey results in the year 2000 found that less than 5% of a teacher's work week was spent on professional learning, and only 1% of teachers spent more than 10% of their work week on these essential activities (Sparks, 2000).

The predominant model of in-service professional development for teachers continues to be the "one-shot" single day workshop, even though there is considerable evidence that such experiences foster little lasting change in teacher practice and generally fail to deliver effective research-based strategies to classrooms (Gersten, Morvant, & Brengelman, 1995; Miller & Lord, 1993). Merely providing teachers with access to innovative instructional strategies through in services is insufficient for altering existing patterns of teaching (Huberman & Miles, 1984;

Richardson, 1994). Furthermore, even when teachers adopt research-based practices, they do not sustain them without significant follow-up training and ongoing, personalized support (Gersten et al., 1995; Gersten, Vaughn, Deshler, & Schiller, 1997; Schumm & Vaughn, 1995).

Several studies show that an essential component to continuing professional development is providing teachers with hands-on practice opportunities with teaching techniques readily applicable to their classroom or in-class demonstrations of specific behaviors that are to be performed (Joyce & Showers, 1988). Hiebert & Taylor (2000) suggest that facilitators in the classroom may be crucial to initiate change in teachers' classroom behavior. Baker and Smith (1999) reported that much of what teachers learn comes from direct classroom experience. Personalized coaching to improve teaching practices has been shown to be effective (Gersten et al., 1995; Showers, 1985).

Summary

In sum, despite increased emphasis in the research literature, as well as national, state, and district policies on the importance of teaching phonological awareness, phonics, and fluent word recognition explicitly and systematically in the general education classroom, studies thus far show that many teachers are not adequately prepared for this task. *Teaching Reading Essentials* addresses this need with a series of video lesson demonstrations ranging in length from 3 to 34 minutes. The lesson demonstrations are designed to model excellent and practical instructional techniques for those teaching beginning reading instruction. The modeled instruction typically addresses the needs of children in grades K through 3. However, some students may progress faster and others will be slower, and the instruction may be necessary for students in grades 3 and up who experience reading problems.

The presentations teach children the various skills associated with phonological awareness, phonics, word recognition, spelling, and reading fluency instruction. Vocabulary, comprehension, and early writing strategies are also demonstrated. These areas of emphasis were selected because a large body of research has documented that these are essential components to reading success, and the lack of skill in these areas is causally linked to reading disability. Furthermore, research clearly demonstrates that students with weaknesses in these areas can progress to the average range if they have effective instruction. The instructional components demonstrated in *Teaching Reading Essentials*, however, are often the areas in which teachers are the least well prepared (NICHD, 2000).

Teaching Reading Essentials provides the characteristics of training that have been shown to be essential for translating content-rich professional development into improvements in reading. Researchers agree that to ensure sustained use of a new approach, the approach must model concrete and practical skills that teachers can integrate with their current teaching repertoires (Gersten et al., 1995; Schumaker, Deshler, & McKnight, 1991; Schumm & Vaughn, 1995). *Teaching Reading Essentials* does not ask teachers to substitute radically different techniques or approaches from those in their core, comprehensive programs. *Teaching Reading Essentials* is practical because the lessons require easy-to-obtain instructional materials that can be found or made at a reasonable cost or for free. *Teaching Reading Essentials* meets the needs of all students by modeling instructional routines that are effective for the typical student learning to read as well as for the student who is low-achieving or with disabilities. Finally, *Teaching Reading*

Essentials provides the opportunity for teachers to learn and hone instructional techniques on their own, in a non-threatening context, after the completion of training workshops.

References

Anders, P., Hoffmann, J. & Duffy, G. (2000). Teaching teachers to teach reading: Paradigm shifts, persistent problems, and challenges. In M. Kamil, P. Mosenthal, P.D. Pearson, & R. Barr (Eds.). *Handbook of Reading Research,* Vol. III , 721-744. Mahwah, NJ: Lawrence Erlbaum Associates.

Baker, S., & Smith, S. (1999). Starting off on the right foot: The influence of four principles of professional development in improving literacy instruction in two kindergarten programs. *Learning Disabilities Research and Practice,* 14(4), 239-253.

Bos, C., Mather, N., Dickson, S., Podhajski, B., & Chard, D. (2001). Perceptions and knowledge of preservice and inservice educators about early reading instruction. *Annals of Dyslexia,* 51, 97–120.

Foorman, B.R., & Moats, L.C. (2004). Conditions for sustaining research-based practices in early reading instruction. *Remedial and Special Education,* 25(1), 51-60.

Foorman, B.R., Schatschnieder, C., Eakin, M.N., Fletcher, J.M., Moats, L.C., & Francis, D.J. (in press). The impact of instructional practices in grades 1 and 2 on reading and spelling achievement in high poverty schools. *Contemporary Educational Psychology.*

Foorman, B.R., Chen, D. T., Carlson, C., Moats, L., Francis, D.J., & Fletcher, J.M. (2003). Necessity of the alphabetic principle to phonemic awareness instruction. *Reading and Writing,* 16, 289-324.

Francis, D. J., Shaywitz, S. E., Stuebing, K. K., Shaywitz, B. A., & Fletcher, J.M. (1996). Developmental lag versus deficit models of reading disability: A longitudinal, individual growth curves analysis. *Journal of Educational Psychology,* 88, 3-17.

Gersten, R., Morvant, M., & Brengelman, S. (1995). Close to the classroom is close to the bone: Coaching as a means to translate research into classroom practice. *Exceptional Children,* 62, 52-66.

Gersten, R., Vaughn, S., Deschler, D., & Schiller, E. (1997). What we know about using research findings: Implications for improving special education practice. *Journal of Learning Disabilities,* 30(5), 466-476.

Hiebert, E. H., & Taylor, B. M. (2000). Beginning reading instruction: Research on early interventions. In R. Barr, M. Kamil, P. Mosenthal, & P. D. Pearson (Eds.), *Handbook of Reading Research* (Vol. 3, pp. 455-482). New York: Longman.

Hill, H. B. (2000). Literacy instruction in teacher education: A comparison of teacher education in Australia, New Zealand, and the United States of America. Unpublished doctoral dissertation, Columbia University, Teaches College, New York.

Huberman, A. M. & Miles, M. (1984). *Innovation up close.* New York: Plenum.

Joyce, B. R., & Showers, B. (1988). *Student achievement through staff development.* White Plains, NY: Longman.

Lyon, R., Vaasen, M., & Toomey, F. (1989). Teachers' perceptions of their undergraduate and graduate preparation. *Teacher Education and Special Education,* 12, 164-169.

Lyon, R. G. (1998). *The NICHD research program in reading development, reading disorders, and reading instruction: A summary of research findings.* Paper presented at the Keys to Successful Learning: A National Summit on Research in Learning Disabilities.

McCutchen, D. & Berninger, V. (1999). Those who know, teach well: Helping teachers master literacy-related subject matter knowledge. *Learning Disabilities Research and Practice,* 14(4), 215-226.

McCutchen, D., Abbott, R.D., Green, L. B., Beretvas, N., Cox, S., Potter, N. S., Quiroga, T., & Gray, A. L. (2002). Beginning literacy: Links among teacher knowledge, teacher practice, and student learning. *Journal of Learning Disabilities,* 1, 69-86.

Miller, B. & Lord, B. (1993). Staff development in four districts. Newton, MA: Educational Development Center.

Moats, L. C. (1994). The missing foundation in teacher education: Knowledge of the structure of spoken and written language. *Annals of Dyslexia,* 44, 81-101.

Moats, L. C. (1995). The missing foundation in teacher education. *American Educator* (Special Issue: Learning to Read: Schooling's First Mission), 19(2), 9, 43-51.

Moats, L.C. (2004). Science, language, and imagination in the professional development of reading teachers. In P. McCardle and V. Chhabra (eds.), *The voice of evidence in reading research* (pp. 269-287). Baltimore: Paul Brookes.

Moats, L. C. & Foorman, B. F. (2003). Measuring teacher's content knowledge of language and reading. *Annals of Dyslexia,* 53, 23-45.

Moats, L. C. & Lyon, G. R. (1996). Wanted: Teachers with knowledge of language. *Topics in Learning Disorders,* 16(2), 73-86.

National Institute of Child Health and Human Development (NICHD) (2000a). *Report of the National Reading Panel. Teaching children to read: An evidence-based assessment of the scientific research literature on reading and its implications for reading instruction.* (NIH Publication No. 00-4769). Washington, DC: United States Government Printing Office. http://www.nichd.nih.gov/publications/nrp/smallbook.htm

National Institute of Child Health and Human Development (NICHD) (2000b). *Report of the National Reading Panel. Teacher children to read: An evidence-based assessment of the scientific research literature on reading and its implications for reading instruction: Reports of the subgroups.* (NIH Publication No. 00-4754). Washington, DC, U.S. Government Printing Office.

O'Conner, R.E. (1999). Teachers learning Ladders to Literacy. *Learning Disabilities Research & Practice,* 14, 203-214.

Rath, L. K. (1994). *The phonemic awareness of reading teachers: Examining aspects of knowledge.* Unpublished doctoral dissertation, Harvard University, Cambridge, MA.

Richardson, V. (1994). *Teacher change and the staff development process.* Teachers College Press.

Share, D. L., & Stanovich, K. E. (1995). Cognitive processes in early reading development: Accommodating individual differences into a model of acquisition. *Issues in Education: Contributions from Educational Psychology,* 1, 1-57.

Schumaker, J. B., Deshler, D. D., & McKnight, P. C. (1991). Teaching routines for content areas at the secondary level. In G. Stoner, M. R. Shinn, & H. M. Walker (Eds.), *Interventions for achievement and behavior problems* (pp. 473-494). Washington, DC: National Association of School Psychologists

Schumm, J.S. & Vaughn, S. (1995). Meaningful professional development in accommodating students with disabilities: Lessons learned. *Remedial and Special Education,* 16(6), 344-353.

Shankweiler, D., Lundquist E., Katz, L., Stuebing, K. K., Fletcher, J. M., Brady, S., et al. (1999). Comprehension and decoding: Patterns of association in children with reading difficulties. *Scientific Studies of Reading,* 3, 69-94.

Showers, B. (1985). Teachers coaching teachers. *Educational Leadership,* 43-48.

Snow, C. E., Griffin, P. & Burns, S. (2006). *Knowledge to Support the Teaching of Reading.* San Francisco: Jossey-Bass.

Sparks, D. & Hirsh, S. (2000). A National Plan for Improving Professional Development. Arlington, VA: National Staff Development Council.

Torgesen, J. K. (2000). Individual differences in response to early interventions in reading: The lingering problem of treatment resisters. *Learning Disabilities Research & Practice,* 15(1), 55-64.

Torgesen, J. K., Alexander, A. W., Wagner, R. K., Rashotte, C. A., Voeller, K., Conway, T., & Rose, E. (2001). Intensive remedial instruction for children with severe reading disabilities: Immediate and long-term outcomes from two instructional approaches. *Journal of Learning Disabilities,* 34, 33-58.

Appendix B: Additional Supplemental Instructional Materials Aligned With *Teaching Reading Essentials*

Phonemic Awareness in Young Children: A Classroom Curriculum. Adams, M.J., Foorman, B.R., Lundberg, I., & Beeler, T. (1998). Baltimore, MD: Brookes Publishing.

Road to The Code: A Phonological Awareness Program for Young Children. Blachman, B.A., Ball, E.W., Black, R., & Tangel, D.M. (2000). Baltimore, MD: Brookes Publishing.

Stepping Stones to Literacy. Nelson, J.R., Cooper, P., & Gonzalez, J. (2004–2005). Longmont, CO: Sopris West.

Building Early Literacy and Language Skills (BELLS). Paulson, L.H., Noble, L.A., Jepson, S., van den Pol, R. (2001). Longmont, CO: Sopris West.

WatchWord. (Grades K-1). Lacey, K., & Baird, W. (2005). Longmont, CO: Sopris West.

Sound Partners. (Grades 1-2). Vadasy, P., Wayne, S., O'Connor, R., Jenkins, J., Pool, K., Firebaugh, M., & Peyton, J. (2005). Longmont, CO: Sopris West.

Phonics and Spelling Through Phoneme-Grapheme Mapping. Grace, K.E.S. (2007). Longmont, CO: Sopris West.

Responsive Reading Instruction: Flexible Intervention for Struggling Readers in the Early Grades. Denton, C.A., & Hocker, J. L. (2006). Longmont, CD: Sopris West.

Spelling by Pattern. (Grades 1-3). Javernick, E. & Moats, L.C. (2007). Longmont, CO: Sopris West.

Spellography. (Grade 4-5). Moats, L.C., & Rosow, B. (2005). Longmont, CO: Sopris West.

Vocabulary Through Morphemes. (Grades 4-6). Ebbers, S.M. (2004). Longmont, CO: Sopris West.

Teacher Resource Manuals

I've DIBEL'd, Now What? Designing Interventions With DIBELS Data. Hall, S. (2006). Longmont, CO: Sopris West.

DIBELS: The Practical Manual. Answers to Questions About Administering, Scoring, and Interpreting DIBELS. Farrell, L., Hancock, C., & Smartt, S. (2006). Longmont, CO: Sopris West.

Appendix C: LETRS Overview

Language Essentials for Teachers of Reading and Spelling (LETRS) is a breakthrough professional development program from Sopris West Educational Services that provides reading coaches, specialists, and teachers with a comprehensive, practical, fad-free understanding of how their students learn to read and write, and spell—and how they can use this understanding to improve and focus instruction.

Years of research and a lifetime of real-world experience with educators went into the development of LETRS. The 12 scientifically based LETRS modules address every component of effective reading instruction—phonological and phonemic awareness; phonics, decoding, spelling and word study; oral language; vocabulary; reading fluency; comprehension; and writing—as well as the foundational concepts of language that link all of the components.

With LETRS, teachers return to the classroom knowing more about the mental processes of reading, and the field-tested instructional strategies that work well for every type of reader.

Module 1 The Challenge of Learning to Read

The first module in the LETRS series explores the reasons why many students have reading difficulties and explains how children learn to read. Case studies illustrate the progression of reading development; the influences of biological, genetic, cognitive, environmental, and instructional factors in learning to read; and the components of effective reading instruction. A "four-part processing system" model is explored in detail.

Module 2 The Speech Sounds of English: Phonetics, Phonology, and Phoneme Awareness

This module introduces phonemes (speech sounds) and discusses the importance of phonological awareness in reading and spelling instruction. Module 2 also discusses the features of consonants and vowels and covers some of the problems that children who speak other languages or dialects may have when learning English.

Module 3 Spellography for Teachers: How English Spelling Works

This module explores the structure and history of English spelling from several angles: phoneme-grapheme correspondences, letter patterns within words, syllables, meaningful word parts (morphemes), and historical layers in the orthography. The module addresses differences between syllables and morphemes, between "irregular" and "high-frequency" words, and among six syllable types. After learning this content, teachers can approach phonics, spelling, and word study with confidence.

Module 4 The Mighty Word: Building Vocabulary

Vocabulary instruction differs from other areas of reading. This module addresses varied approaches to instruction, including indirect (contextual) and direct methodologies, and stressing techniques for fostering word use, knowledge of word relationships, and awareness of word structure and its connection to meaning. Participants apply what they have learned about vocabulary instruction to several examples of narrative and expository text.

Module 5 Getting Up to Speed: Developing Fluency

Comprehensive reading instruction includes deliberate fluency building at the subword, word, phrase, and text levels for those students who read too slowly. This module reviews the rationale for a fluency component in lesson design. Participants learn and practice techniques for speed drills, repeated reading, simultaneous and alternate oral reading, calculating reading fluency, and charting the results of exercises.

Module 6 Digging for Meaning: Teaching Text Comprehension

Comprehension instruction is one of the most researched areas in reading education, yet it is also one of the most challenging. This module addresses the research base for teaching comprehension, the reasons why children have difficulty with comprehension, and approaches for teaching comprehension at the phrase, sentence, paragraph, and passage levels. Questioning techniques and strategies that are useful before, during, and after reading are reviewed. Exercises include text analysis for planning instruction.

Module 7 Teaching Phonics, Word Study, and the Alphabetic Principle

Effective, enjoyable, systematic phonics instruction involves many subroutines that are all practiced in this module. The sequence and substance of concept development in code-based instruction is emphasized, including the importance of applying learned skills to reading and writing. Answers to common questions are provided, including "How Much Phonics?", "Who Needs Phonics?", "What Kind of Phonics?", and "Why Phonics?".

Module 8 Assessment for Prevention and Early Intervention

In this module, screening and progress monitoring assessments are distinguished from diagnostic and outcome assessment. The rationale for early screening with fluency-based measures is reviewed. DIBELS is used as the example of a valid, reliable, efficient approach to early screening. A developmental spelling inventory is taught. Exercises include review of classroom reports and individual case studies in light of children's instructional needs and the "three-tier" concept of intervention.

Module 9 Teaching Beginning Spelling and Writing

This module addresses writing instruction for children in grades K-2 who need to be taught the component skills that underlie composition. Drawing on recent research at the University of Washington that explicates the cognitive and linguistic components of composition skill, a framework for analyzing writing samples is applied to several examples of students at different levels of achievement. Instruction that builds automaticity in critical components while teaching children the stages of the writing process is explained and modeled.

Module 10 Reading Big Words: Syllabication and Advanced Decoding

Module 10 addresses the instructional needs of students in grades 3 and up who are inaccurate and/or slow in reading and spelling multisyllabic words. Beginning with phoneme-grapheme mapping, the module goes on to address systematic teaching of syllabication, syllable spelling types, and ending rules. Morphology — including inflections, Anglo Saxon compounds, Latin and Greek roots and affixes, and derivational word learning processes — is addressed in some depth. An Advanced Decoding Survey is included with this module along with lists of instructional resources and programs.

Module 11 Writing: A Road to Reading Comprehension

If students actively seek, organize, and reformulate information in their own words, their reading comprehension is likely to improve. Module 11, designed for all classroom and content area teachers, presents a few major strategies that help students process and remember the main ideas in written text. Additionally, it reviews the many causes of reading comprehension difficulties and addresses the research consensus on teaching reading comprehension. Text structure and its relation to comprehension are explored, and participants learn to implement the Key Three Routine, to include construction of topic organizers, note-taking, and summarizing. A list of effective curriculum materials for teaching older students to read and write is included in the module.

Module 12 Using Assessment to Guide Instruction

Module 12 is an advanced module for intermediate and middle school educators to help them identify and pinpoint the instructional needs of all struggling readers. The module describes efficient, reliable, and research-based assessment strategies that enable a school staff to focus on the effectiveness of instruction. Participants review a strategic plan for screening students and learn how to assemble a group of suitable assessments for individual and classroom use. Diagnostic tests that measure decoding and word analysis, spelling, written composition, reading fluency, and comprehension are demonstrated and rehearsed. Case studies allow participants to discuss and analyze assessment results and their implications.

Appendix D: The Sequence of English Phoneme Awareness Development

Many studies of phonological development point to the following benchmarks for children's progress in this critical skill.[1] Children's performance on phonological tasks can be accelerated through direct teaching and practice. The age at which they consolidate skill will depend, however, on language exposure prior to school, home language context, familiarity with letter-sound correspondence, and overall verbal proficiency.

Phoneme Awareness Benchmarks Between Ages 4–9

Typical Age Attained	Skill Domain	Sample Tasks
4	Enjoyment of rhyme and alliteration.	Pool, drool, tool … Seven silly snakes sang songs seriously.
5	Rhyming, odd word out.	Which two words rhyme? *stair, steel, chair*
	Recognition of phonemic changes in words.	*"Hickory Dickory Clock"* isn't right. What should it be?
	Tapping or counting syllables.	*truck (1),* *airplane (2), boat(1),* *automobile (4)*
5.5	Distinguishing and remembering separate phonemes in a series.	Showing sequences of single phonemes with colored blocks */s/ /s/ /f/; /z/ /sh/ /z/.*
	Blending onset and rime.	What word? *th-under;* *qu-een; h-appy*
	Rhyme production	What word rhymes with *mess?*
	Segmenting initial sound.	Say the first sound in *shoelace; sock; funnel.*

[1] Numerous studies suggest a predictable sequence of phonological skill development. Syntheses and overviews of those studies can be found in these two chapters: Rath, L. (2001). Phonemic awareness. In S. Brody (ed.), *Teaching Reading: Language, Letters, and Thought.* Milford, NH: LARC Publishing; Goswami, U. (2000). Phonological and lexical processes. In M. L. Kamil, P. B. Mosenthal, P. D. Pearson, & R. Barr (eds.), *Handbook of reading research.* Mahwah, NJ: Lawrence Erlbaum Associates. The sequence is embodied in M. J. Adams, B. R. Foorman, I. Lundberg, & T. Beeler. (1997). *Phonemic Awareness in Young Children: A Classroom Curriculum.* Baltimore, MD: Brookes Publishing Co.

Typical Age Attained	Skill Domain	Sample Tasks
6	Syllable deletion	Say *parsnip*; say it again but don't say *par.*
	Compound word deletion.	Say *cowboy.* Say it again but don't say *cow.*
	Onset-rime blending; beginning phoneme blending.	/sh/-op (shop) /kw/-ēn (queen) /b/-āth (bathe) /b/-/ā/-/th/ (bathe)
	Phoneme segmentation, simple syllables with 2–3 phonemes [no blends].	Say the word as you move a chip for each sound: *sh-e, m-a-n, l-e-g*
6.5	Phoneme segmentation up to 3–4 phonemes, including blends	Say the word slowly while you tap the sounds: b–a–ck; ch–ee–se; c-l-ou-d
	Phoneme substitution to build new words—simple syllables with no blends.	Change the /j/ in *cage* to /n/. Change the /ā/ in *cane* to /ō/.
7	Sound deletion, initial and final position.	Say *meat.* Say it again without the /m/. Say *safe.* Say it again without the /f/.
8	Sound deletion, initial position, including blends.	Say *prank.* Now say it again without the /p/.
9	Sound deletion, medial and final blend position.	Say *snail.* Say it again without the /n/. Say *fork.* Say it again without the /k/.

150

Teaching Reading Essentials

Appendix E: Guide Words and Gestures

Guide Words and Gestures for Consonant Sounds

Consonant Sounds	Guide Word/Picture	Gesture
/b/	ball	Bounce a ball.
/p/	pencil	Pretend to write with a pencil.
/m/	/mmmmm/ (monkey rubbing tummy)	Rub your tummy.
/d/	dig (person digging big hole)	Pretend to dig a hole.
/t/	ten (number 10)	Hold up ten fingers.
/n/	nose	Touch your nose.
/g/	gum	Pretend to chew gum.
/k/	cat (with claws)	Make hands like claws.
/sh/	/shshshsh/ (finger in front of mouth)	Put finger in front of mouth.
/ng/	sing (person with mouth open; bubble with notes floating in it)	Sing a note and hold the /ng/ sound.
/f/	fan (electric fan)	Fan your face with your hand.
/v/	hand with the v sign	Make a victory sign with your hand.
/th/	thumb	Hold up a thumb.
/th/	that	Point to something and say /th/.
/s/	snake	Make a winding snake movement with hand.
/z/	zipper	Pretend to zip up a jacket.
/j/	jar	Pretend to open a jar.
/ch/	chin	Point to your chin.
/y/	yes! (person with hands up in y shape)	Hold hands overhead in y shape and pull down.
/w/	wave (person waving good-bye)	Wave good-bye.
/h/	hat	Tip your hat.
/l/	leg	Point to your leg.
/r/	rabbit	Make rabbit ears.

Adapted from Javernick, E., & Moats, L. C. (2007). *Spelling by Pattern*. Longmont, CO: Sopris West.

Guide Words and Gestures for Vowel Sounds

Vowel Sounds	Guide Word/Picture	Gesture
/ē/ (long e)	eagle	
/ĭ/ (short i)	itching (scratch an itch)	Scratch an itch.
/ā/ (long a)	apron	
/ĕ/ (short e)	echo (picture of person with hands to mouth)	Put your hands to your mouth and say "e-cho."
/ă/ (short a)	apple	Sweep a hand across your body as if an apple were in your palm.
/ī/ (long i)	ice cream (ice cream cone)	
/ŏ/ (short o)	octopus	Sweep a hand across your body like an octopus swimming, using fingers for tentacles.
/ŭ/ (short u)	up (arrow pointing up)	Point up with finger.
/aw/	*aw, shucks!* (upside down ice cream cone splattered on pavement)	Shake your head and say /aw/.
/ō/ (long o)	oval	
/o͝o/	look (picture of glasses drawn around the "oo")	Hold hands up to your eyes to mime looking.
/o͞o/ (unglided long u)	new moon	
/yu/ (glided long u)	unicorn	
/oi/ (diphthong)	oink (picture of pig saying *oink!*)	
/ou/	*ow!* (person pinching self and saying *ow!*)	
/er/	*brrr* (person shivering)	

Adapted from Javernick, E., & Moats, L. C. (2007). *Spelling by Pattern*. Longment, CO: Sopris West.

Appendix F: *Responsive Reading Instruction*

Carolyn Denton and Jennifer Hocker

Responsive Reading Instruction: Flexible Intervention for Struggling Readers in the Early Grades (Sopris West, 2006) was created to help the lowest-performing first and second graders learn to read competently and within the average range for their age groups. *Responsive Reading Instruction* (RRI) is grounded in years of research; in fact, a study comparing RRI's effectiveness with that of a more scripted intervention program showed that it was equally powerful in "closing the reading gap."[1] The number of children experiencing reading failure after intervention with each program was reduced from to 2%. The study documenting this rate of success received the Albert Harris award from the International Reading Association in 2006.

Lessons are taught to small groups of 3-5 children on a daily basis. Each 40-minute lesson is based on six elements shown to be important in effective reading instruction:

- **Instruction in key domains of reading**—phonemic awareness, phonics, fluency, vocabulary, comprehension, and writing skills.

- **Explicit instruction**—RRI uses a lesson format that explicitly teaches students the basic skills needed to decode words and read text with understanding.

- **Opportunities to practice**—specially-designed activities give struggling students as many chances as they need to automatize what they have learned.

- **Targeted instruction based on assessment**—RRI teachers are able to focus intervention on trouble areas using individual student assessments.

- **Scaffolding and feedback**—RRI teachers provide supports to enable reading success. Both accuracy and fluency in word recognition, essential for building reading confidence, are fostered.

- **The home connection**—teachers work closely with parents to support a positive attitude toward reading.

Responsive Reading Instruction allows the trained teacher to formulate daily lesson plans within a framework of teaching principles and lesson components. It can be taught with decodable texts (for beginning readers) and, later, texts that are less controlled. The accompanying DVD presents actual classroom instruction that demonstrates how to implement many of the RRI activites.

---

[1] Mathes P. G., Denton, C.A., Flectcher, J.M., Anthony, J. L., Francis, D. J. & Schatschneider, C. (2005) *The effects of theoretically different instruction and student characteristics on the skills of struggling readers.* Reading Research Quarterly. *40*(2), 148–182.

Appendix G: Targeted Reading Lessons

Linda Farrell and Michael Hunter
Really Great Reading Company, forthcoming in 2007

Targeted Reading Lessons, the foundation of the *Teaching Reading Essentials* phonics lessons, are designed for flexible use in reading intervention programs. The philosophy of *Targeted Reading Lessons* is that teachers can more effectively help students to read when students' specific reading weaknesses are identified and lessons are structured around those weaknesses. Really Great Reading Company's *Reading Skills Surveys* will give teachers information about students' specific weaknesses, which can be mapped to one or more of the *Targeted Reading Lessons.*

Targeted Reading Lessons address phonological awareness, letter names and sounds, and various levels of phonics skills. An informal mastery assessment is provided for each skill taught so that students do not move on until they have mastered the skill. Assessments are also provided at the end of each book. Each of the ten *Targeted Reading Lessons* books, with its contents, is described below.

Book A: Phonological Awareness

Book B: Phonemic Awareness

Book C: Letter Names and Sounds

Book D: High Frequency Words

Book E: Beginning Phonics—Short Vowels

Book F: Intermediate Phonics—Short Vowels

Book G: Advanced Phonics #1—Silent E and R-contolled Vowels

Book H: Advanced Phonics #2—Long Vowels with Multiple Spellings

Book I: Advanced Phonics #3—Other Vowels with Multiple Spellings

Book J: Rounding Out Reading

Targeted Reading Lessons are currently in development and are scheduled to be available by Spring, 2007. Updated information about *Targeted Reading Lessons* can be found at the Really Great Reading Company Web site, http://www.reallygreatreading.com.

Appendix H: Books to Support Phonics Reading

Decodable phonics readers help students apply the decoding skills they have been directly taught. Many novice readers benefit from such practice. Phonics readers help students avoid guesswork and establish the habit of sounding out words they do not know.

Bob Books
Scholastic, Inc.
http://www.scholastic.com

Books to Remember
Flyleaf Publishing Co.
(603) 795-2875
http://www.flyleafpublishing.com

Dr. Maggie's Phonics Readers
(75-80% decodable)
Perfection Learning
http://www.perfectionlearning.com/maggie/

Orton-Gillingham Reader Books I & II
Elena Winter
3 Hearthwood Drive, Barrington, RI 02806

EZ2 Read Decodable Books
Barbara Nicholson Books
(888) 521-4080
http://www.ez2read.com

Garside Readers
Garside Institute
(718) 259-8342

Get Ready, Get Set, Read! Series
Barron's Educational Series, Inc.
(800) 645-3476
http://www.barronseduc.com

Go Phonics Decodable Storybooks
Foundations for Learning, LLC
(800) 553-5950
http://www.gophonics.com

High Noon Books
Academic Therapy Publications
(800) 422-7249
http://www.academictherapy.com

Phonics Funnies
Sopris West Educational Services
(800) 547-6747
http://www.sopriswest.com

Phonics Practice Readers
Modern Curriculum Press
(800) 876-5507
http://www.pearsonlearning.com/mcschool/

Phonics Readers
Educational Insights
(800) 995-4436
http://www.edin.com

Phonics Readers
Steck-Vaughn (a Harcourt company)
(800) 531-5015
http://www.steck-vaughn.com

Phonemic Awareness and Sequencing (P.A.S.) Stories
AGS American Guidance Service
(800) 471-8457
http://www.agsnet.com

Poppin Auditory Discrimination Reading Series: Sound by Sound Stories
Pro-Ed Publishers
http://www.proed.com

Power Readers
Sopris West Educational Services
(303) 651-2829
http://www.sopriswest.com

Readers at Work
Readers at Work
http://www.readersatwork.com

Primary Phonics and More Primary Phonics; Alphabet Series, Volumes 1 and 2
Educators Publishing Service, Inc.
(800) 435-7728
http://www.epsbooks.com

Reading for All Learners Program
read@cc.usu.edu
(435) 797-1120

Reading Rods Readers Phonics Foundation Sets
http://www.etacuisenaire.com
1-800-445-5985

Sundance Phonics
Sundance Publishing
(800) 343-8204
http://www.sundancepub.com

Step Into Success: Short Vowel Books – High Interest Stories; Sound Out Chapter Book Series
Reading and Language Arts Center
The Ultimate Multisensory Product Catalog
http://www.rlac.com
(886) 307-0802

Reading Sparkers
Children's Research & Development Co.
(609) 546-9896

Rigby Decodable Stories
Rigby Education
(800) 822-8661
http://www.rigby.com

The Wright Skills Decodable Books
The Wright Group
(800) 523-2371
http://www.wrightgroup.com

SRA/McGraw-Hill Options:
(890) SRA-4543
www.sra4kids.com

- **Open Court Phonics Minibooks Grades 1-3**
  (Collections for Young Scholars 1995)
- **Open Court Decodable Books Grades 1 – 3**
  (Orange 2000 version)
- **Merrill Reading Program Student Readers Grades 1-3**
- **SRA Phonics: Grade 1-3**
  Poetry Posters containing vowels, blends, and digraphs
- **Independent Readers for students in Reading Mastery I and II: Grade 1-3**
  Print matches Reading mastery unique alphabet

Appendix I: General Lesson Plan for Beginning Reading Instruction: Introducing Multiple Spellings for One Sound

Linda Farrell and Michael Hunter

1. Phonemic Warm-up

- Students identify phonemes in words with target sounds.
- Students identify whether the vowel sounds in words are short, long, or neither.

2. Heart and Flash Words

- Students read and spell current heart and flash words. Words are retired after a student reads and spells them correctly three times in a row.
- At least once a month, students (1) engage in a timed reading of 10 to 15 words selected from their "retired" words and (2) spell at least 5 of the retired words.

3. Review Prior Lesson's Concept – include any other concepts that need review

4. Teach New Concept

- Tell students the sound that is being taught and have them repeat it.
- Use letter tiles to introduce the various spellings for the sound.
  - Show students each spelling for the sound being taught by spelling the guide word with letter tiles.
  - Have students in the group chorally say each sound in the word as you touch each letter tile.
  - Ask how the target sound is spelled in that word.
  - Repeat until all spellings have been introduced.
- After all spellings have been introduced, cover the spellings and have students:
  - Write each spelling and the guide word on the white board, underlining the target spelling in the guide word.
  - Hold their white boards up when they have finished so teacher can check.
  - Write the spellings on their guide word chart.

5. Reinforce Concept — Use one or more of the following activities:

- Sort words by spelling of target sound.
- Read word list, underlining spelling for target sound in each word.
- Read word pattern lists
- Read multisyllabic word lists.

6. Fluency Practice — Use one or more of the following activities:

- Read word lists, including timed and repeated readings.
- Read phrases, including timed and repeated readings.
- Read decodable sentences, including timed and repeated readings.

7. Spelling

- Use the spelling grid by selecting words that have been used in the lesson and having students write the words in the appropriate column.
- Dictate sentences.

8. Read Connected Text

Accuracy — Read decodable text or leveled readers until students read with 98% accuracy.

Fluency — After students achieve 98% accuracy, have them read orally for one minute and record the number of words read correctly. Have students re-read the decodable or leveled readers, sometimes with timed readings.

Comprehension — Ask questions after students read for accuracy or fluency or have students retell or summarize passages.

Appendix J

The Informal Reading Surveys are designed to pinpoint a student's specific weaknesses at different levels of reading development. Information from the surveys tells teachers exactly where to begin instruction with a student. The surveys can also be used to group students with the same instructional needs.

REALLY GREAT READING COMPANY (www.reallygreatreading.com or 866-401-7323) sells the complete set of surveys that includes: (i) 5 forms of the surveys at each level that can be used for progress monitoring; (ii) complete, detailed directions; (iii) information for interpreting the surveys; and (iv) class grouping charts.

This sample set was prepared specifically for *Teaching Reading Essentials*. It contains one survey with summary directions for each of the reading and pre-reading levels listed below:

Beginning Decoding Survey
- Use this survey to begin assessment of all students in the middle of first grade or older.
- The Beginning Decoding Survey shows whether students have mastered basic decoding skills that enable them to accurately read words with short vowels. It also includes several high frequency words.
- The Error Pattern Grid shows the specific areas in which the student needs instruction.

Advanced Decoding Survey
- As a general guideline, use this survey for students who miss 0 - 5 words on the Beginning Decoding Survey.
- The nonsense words have various vowel spelling patterns and some have more than one syllable. The ability to read these words shows whether the student can decode unfamiliar words with these spelling patterns.
- Real multi-syllabic words are included so that the assessor can compare the difference between the student's ability to read unfamiliar and familiar words.
- The Error Pattern Grid shows the specific areas in which the student needs instruction.

Phonological Awareness Survey
- Use this survey for students who perform poorly on the Beginning Decoding Survey. A general guideline is to use this survey for students who miss 15 or more words on the Beginning Decoding Survey.
- Also use this survey for children in kindergarten or 1st grade suspected of having difficulties learning to read.
- The Phonological Awareness Survey shows whether students can orally blend syllables and onset & rime into words and whether they can identify and match oral initial and final sounds in words.
- Students who score *emerging* or *low* in any category on this survey need instruction in that skill.

Phonemic Awareness Survey
- Use this survey for students who have no *low* scores and no more than 2 *emerging* scores on the Phonological Awareness Survey.
- This survey can also be useful in kindergarten and first grade as a screening instrument to identify students who have phonemic awareness weaknesses and need extra instruction.
- The Phonemic Awareness Survey shows whether students can blend and segment 3 or 4 sounds in words.
- Students who score *emerging* or *low* in any category on this survey need instruction in that skill.

Letter Name and Letter Sound Survey
- Use this survey for students who perform poorly on the Beginning Decoding Survey. A general guideline is to use both sections of this survey for students who miss 15 or more words on the Beginning Decoding Survey.
- Another guideline is to give only the Letter Sound Survey to students who have more than 5 errors in any one error pattern column on the Beginning Decoding Survey.
- The Letter Name and Letter Sound Surveys show whether students know their letter names and letter sounds.
- Students need to be taught any letter names or sounds that they do not know.
- Expect many students who perform poorly on the Beginning Decoding Survey to need instruction in short vowel sounds, the sounds for certain consonants - especially g, y, w, x, qu – and the sounds for the digraphs ch, sh, th, wh.

Beginning Decoding Survey

Summary Directions

More detailed directions are included in the User's Guide, available at www.ReallyGreatReading.com.

Instructions for Administering Survey
Student reads words and sentences on *Words and Sentences to Read* page.
When the student misreads a word, assessor writes <u>exactly</u> what the student reads on the *Recording Form and Error Grid*.

- Show the *Words and Sentences to Read* page to the student.
- Explain that the student is to read the words and sentences.
- Emphasize the following:
    - Accuracy is more important than fluency
    - The student may take as much time as needed
    - The student may say, "I don't know the word."
- Ask the student to read words and sentences from <u>left to right</u>, one set at a time.
    - If an assessor finds it hard to keep pace with the student reading the words, the assessor may use a piece of paper to reveal one line of words at a time.
- Identify the nonsense words as such before the student reads them.

Recording Instructions
- Use the *Recording Form and Error Grid*.
- Place a check (√) mark next to words read correctly.
- If student misreads a word, write <u>exactly</u> what the student reads next to the word.
- If the student misreads a word more than once, write <u>all</u> attempts that are not correct.
- If the student self corrects, record <u>all</u> incorrect responses and note the self correction by writing "SC". Self corrections are <u>not</u> counted in the Total Words Correct.
- If the student makes no attempt or says "I don't know," cross out the word and place an X in the "No Try" column.
- When the student reads sentences, place a check mark (√) above each word read correctly. If a word is misread, cross out the word and write exactly what the student read above the misread word.
- Check the appropriate boxes in the "Observations" section to indicate whether the student read sound by sound and then blended the word, was quick to guess, possibly made a b/d reversal, or was slow.
- Write observations about student's behavior in the "Comments" space or on back of the *Recording Form and Error Grid*.

Error Pattern Grid Instructions
- <u>After</u> you have finished giving the survey, analyze the errors and place an X in the appropriate boxes in the error pattern grid for each part of the word read incorrectly.
    - Each misread word may have one or more boxes with X's in them.
- For errors in the sentences, place X's in the appropriate boxes for all errors. Boxes may have more than one X in them to indicate the same error was made twice in a sentence.
- Be sure to include the errors in responses made before a self correction.
- See User's Guide for more details about scoring, analyzing errors, and interpreting results.

2

Student _____   Grade _____   Age _____   Date _____

Assessor _____

		Real Words	No Try	Sight Word	**Error Patterns**

Error Patterns

Observations: check the appropriate boxes

Reads sound by sound, then blends word ☐

Possible b/d reversal ☐

Quick to guess ☐

Slow ☐

Add Comments on Back

		Real Words	No Try	Sight Word	Added or Omitted	Initial	Final	Short Vowels	
High Frequency Words	1	see							
	2	one							
	3	play							
	4	you							
	5	are							
CVC Words	6	rag							
	7	lid							
	8	dot							Digraphs: ch, sh, ck, wh, th. or letters qu
	9	hum							
	10	bet							
Digraphs & Short Vowels	11	rich							
	12	shop							
	13	tack							
	14	quit							
	15	thin							Blends
Blends & Short Vowels	16	dust							
	17	step							
	18	trip							
	19	pond							
	20	brag							

Sentences (irregularly spelled sight words in *italics*)

21 - 26	1. *The* cat hid in *a* box.	
27 - 35	2. *The* fresh fish *is* still on *the* wet grass.	
36 - 42	3. Six pink shells *were* in *my* bath.	

Nonsense Words

			No Try	Sight Word	Added or Omitted	Initial	Final	Short Vowels	
CVC	43	vop							
	44	yug							
	45	zin							
	46	keb							
Digraphs	47	shap							
	48	thid							
	49	chut							
	50	wheck							

Words Correct: _____ /50 |Column Totals:

Form A

Words and Sentences to Read

Set #1

see	one	play	you	are
rag	lid	dot	hum	bet
rich	shop	tack	quit	thin
dust	step	trip	pond	brag

Set #2

1. The cat hid in a box.

2. The fresh fish is still on the wet grass.

3. Six pink shells were in my bath.

Set #3

vop	yug	zin	keb
shap	thid	chut	wheck

4

Advanced Decoding Survey

Summary Directions

More detailed directions are included in the User's Guide, available at ww.ReallyGreatReading.com.

Instructions for Administering Survey
The student reads nonsense and real words on *Words to Read* page.
When the student misreads a word, assessor writes <u>exactly</u> what the student reads on *Recording Form and Error Grid*.

- Show the student the *Words to Read* page.
- Explain that the student is to read the words.
- Explain that the words in the first three sets are nonsense words and the words in the last set are real words.
- Emphasize the following:
  - Accuracy is more important than fluency.
  - The student may take as much time as needed.
  - The student may say, "I don't know the word."
- Ask the student to read words from <u>left to right</u>, one set at a time.
  - If an assessor is finding it hard to keep pace with the student reading the words, then the assessor may use a piece of paper to reveal one line of words at a time.

Recording Instructions
- Use the *Recording Form and Error Grid*.
- Place a check mark (√) next to words read correctly.
- If the student misreads a word, write <u>exactly</u> what the student reads next to the word.
- If the student misreads a word more than once, write <u>all</u> attempts that are not correct.
- If the student self corrects, record <u>all</u> incorrect responses and note the self correction by writing "SC". Self corrections are <u>not</u> counted in the Total Words Correct.
- If the student makes no attempt or says "I don't know," cross out the word and place an X in the "No Try" column.
- Check the appropriate boxes in the "Observations" section to indicate whether the student read sound by sound and then blended the word, was quick to guess, possibly made a b/d reversal, or was slow.
- Write observations about the student's behavior in the "Comments" section or on back of the *Recording Form and Error Grid*.

Error Pattern Grid Instructions
- <u>After</u> you have finished giving the survey, analyze the errors and place an X in the appropriate boxes in the error pattern grid for each part of the word read incorrectly.
  - Each misread word may have one or more boxes with X's in them.
- Be sure to include the errors in responses made before a self correction.
- See User's Guide for more details about analyzing errors and interpreting results.

5

Advanced Decoding Skills Survey Recording Form and Error Grid Form A

Student _____ Grade _____ Age _____ Date _____

Assesor _____

Error Patterns

Observations — Check the appropriate boxes:

Reads sound by sound, then blends word ☐
Possible b/d reversal ☐
Quick to guess ☐
Slow ☐

Notes:

	Nonsense Words	no try	added, omitted, reversed	consonants initial	consonants final	short vowels & schwa	consonant digraphs: sh, ch, th, ph, trigraphs: dge & tch			
1	fut									
2	shap									
3	thox									
4	lutch									
5	phid							blends		
6	gred									
7	strup							long vowels		
8	misp									
9	weaf									
10	jaib									
11	yume								other vowels	
12	voe									
13	voop									
14	awk									
15	soid									
16	zout									
17	foy									vowel +r
18	fird									
19	gorf									
20	lerm									

one syllable & one vowel: 1–8
vowel teams: 9–17
vowel +r: 18–20

Error Column Totals:

	Multi-syllabic Words	no try	misread
21	complut		
22	gruckle		
23	slafnode		
24	dirper		
25	panventic		
	Real Words		
26	wrecker		
27	alive		
28	forgotten		
29	several		
30	refreshing		
31	fantastic		
32	demonstrate		
33	lotion		

multisyllable: 21–25
multi syllable real: 26–33

General Comments:

Total Words Correct: _____/33   ⇐ Multisyllabic Word Error Totals

6

Words to Read

Nonsense Words

Set #1

fut	shap	thox
lutch	phid	gred
strup	misp	

Set #2

weaf	jaib	yume
voe	voop	awk
soid	zout	foy
fird	gorf	lerm

Set #3

complut	gruckle	slafnode
dirper	panventic	

Real Words

wrecker	alive	forgotten
several	refreshing	fantastic
demonstrate	lotion	

ADS

7

Letter Sounds and Letter Names Survey

Summary Directions

More detailed directions are included in the User's Guide, available at www.ReallyGreatReading.com.

Instructions for Administering Survey

The *Recording and Scoring Form* and the *Letter Sounds and Letter Names* Student Page are set up for both letter sounds and letter names. The assessor can give either or both surveys.

- Show the student the appropriate half of the *Letter Names and Letter Sounds* Student Page.
- Explain that the student is to say the <u>sound</u> or <u>name</u>, whichever is appropriate, for each of the letters.
- Emphasize the following:
  - Accuracy is more important than fluency
  - Student may say, "I don't know the sound."

For letter <u>sounds</u>, the student gives sounds for the letters on the top half of the *Letter Sounds and Letter Names* Student Page.

For the vowel letters:
- The desired answer is the short vowel sound.
- If the student gives a correct long vowel sound, say: *"(Letter name) does spell that sound. Do you know any others sounds for that letter?"*
- If the student gives an incorrect long vowel sound, say: *"Do you know any others sounds for that letter?"*

For the consonant letters **c** and **g**:
- The desired answer is the hard sound: /k/ for **c** and /g/ for **g.**
- If the student gives the correct soft sound, say: *"(Letter name) does spell that sound. Do you know any others sounds for that letter?"*

For letter <u>names</u>, the student gives names for the letters on the bottom half of the *Letter Sounds and Letter Names* Student Page.

When the student gives an incorrect answer, assessor writes <u>exactly</u> what the student says on *Recording and Scoring Form*.

Recording Instructions
- Place a check mark (√) on the *Recording and Scoring Form* next to letters for which the correct response is given.
- If the student gives an incorrect response, write the student's <u>exact</u> response next to the letter.
- For letter <u>sounds</u> - If the student gives a letter name, record the name as given. Then say: *"That is a letter name, do you know the sound for that letter?"*
- For letter <u>names</u> - If the student gives a letter sound, record the sound as given. Then say: *"That is a letter sound, do you know the name for that letter?"*
- If the student misreads a letter more than once, write <u>all</u> attempts that are not correct.
- If the student self corrects, record <u>all</u> the incorrect sound(s) or name(s) given and note the self correction by writing "SC".
- If the student makes no attempt or says "I don't know," cross out the letter and write "NT" next to the letter for "no try."
- For letter <u>sounds</u> - Be sure to note when the student adds the sound /uh/ to a letter sound.
- Write observations about the student's behavior in the Comments section.

Scoring Instructions
- <u>After</u> you have finished giving the survey, count the letters with a check mark (√) and enter the total in the appropriate scoring box for letter sounds or letter names. Self corrections are <u>not</u> counted as correct answers.
- Highlight or circle the appropriate skill level in the Skill Level boxes for letter sounds or letter names.

Option to Survey Printing Skills
- There is the option for the student to print upper and lower case letters, with space provided for scoring.

8

Letter Sounds and Letter Names Survey　　　　　　　　　　　　　　**Form A**

Recording and Scoring Form

Name _____ Grade _____ Age _____ Date_____

Assesor: _____

Letter Sounds

						Number Correct
a	e	i	o	u		
c	b	g	n	j		
l	m	r	s	v		
w	f	y	z	p		
k	x	d	h	t		
ch	sh	ck	wh	th	qu	

Comments:

	Skill Level		Number Correct
Low	Emerging	Established	
0-21	21-28	29-31	/31

Letter Names

						Number Correct
a	e	i	o	u		
c	b	g	n	j		
l	m	r	s	v		
w	f	y	z	p		
k	x	d	h	t	q	

Comments:

	Skill Level		Number Correct
Low	Emerging	Established	
0-16	16-23	25-26	/26

Optional Letter Writing Upper Case

Letters Missed

Comments:

	Skill Level		Number Correct
Low	Emerging	Established	
0-16	16-23	25-26	/26

Optional Letter Writing Lower Case

Letters Missed

Comments:

	Skill Level		Number Correct
Low	Emerging	Established	
0-16	16-23	25-26	/26

Letter Sounds Survey

Say the **sound** for each letter.

a	e	i	o	u
c	b	g	n	j
l	m	r	s	v
w	f	y	z	p
k	x	d	h	t

ch	sh	ck	wh	th	qu

Letter Name Survey

Say the **name** for each letter.

a	e	i	o	u
c	b	g	n	j
l	m	r	s	v
w	f	y	z	p
k	x	d	h	t	q

10

Phonological Awareness Survey

Summary Directions

More detailed directions are included in the *User's Guide*, available at www.ReallyGreatReading.com.

Instructions for Administering Survey
On the *Recording and Scoring Form* put a check (√) next to any correct answers.
When the student makes an error, write <u>exactly</u> what the student reads on the *Recording and Scoring Form* in the space provided.
If the student does not attempt an answer, write "NT" for "no try."

<u>Blending Word Parts</u> – Use the 2 boxes on *Student Page 1*.
- Assessor orally says each part of the word, pausing 2 seconds between syllables.
- The student blends word parts into words.

Compound words, 2 syllable words, and onset/rime
- Demonstrate with the practice word **rainbow**:
    - Say: ***"I am going to say two parts of a word. You put the parts together and tell me what the whole word is. Let's do a sample together.* Rain** (pause 2 seconds) **bow."** Touch the box on the student's left when you say **rain** and the one on the student's right when you say **bow**.
    - Say: ***"When I put the parts together, they make one word – rainbow."*** Place your hand flat between the 2 boxes to show blending the 2 parts.
    - Say: ***"Now let's do it together."*** Have the student follow you using the same procedure.
    - Say: ***"Now it's your turn to put some word parts together. You can touch the boxes to help."***
- Read the word parts for each compound word on the *Recording and Scoring Form*, touching the boxes as above.
- Read the word parts for each two syllable word on the *Recording and Scoring Form*, touching the boxes as above.
- Read the onset and rime for each word on the *Recording and Scoring Form*, touching the boxes as above.
- (If any part is too difficult for the student, discontinue and go on to Matching Initial Phonemes.)

<u>Matching Initial Phonemes</u> - Use the pictures at the top of *Student Page 2*.
- Demonstrate with the practice word **moon**:
    - Point to each of the four pictures as you say their names (listed on the *Recording and Scoring Form*) and have the student repeat the name of each picture.
    - Point to the picture of the moon and say: ***"/m/ is the first sound in* moon. *Say /m/."*** After the student says /m/, say: ***"Which picture here has the same first sound as* moon?"** (The student can point to the picture or name it.)
    - If the student points to the correct picture (mouse), say: ***"Yes,* mouse *has the same first sound as* moon."***
    - If the student does not point to the correct picture (mouse), say: ***"Mmmmouse* starts with the sound /m/, just like mmmmoon *starts with the sound /m/. Say* mmmmoon.** (The student repeats mmmmoon.) ***Say* mmmmouse."** (The student repeats mmmmouse.)
- Say: ***"You do the next three by yourself. I'll tell you the names of the pictures. This is* (point to and name the first picture)."** (Pictures are named on the *Recording and Scoring Form*.)
- Point to and name the next three pictures. Say: ***"Which one begins with the same sound as* (name the first picture in the row)."**
- Repeat for the next two words.

Identifying Initial Phonemes - Use pictures in the last row on *Student Page 2*.
- Demonstrate with the practice word **soap**:
  - Point to the first picture and say: *"This is* **soap***. What is the first sound in the word* **soap***?"*
  - If the student correctly names the sound /s/, say: *"Yes, the first sound in* **soap** *is /s/."*
  - If the student does not name the sound /s/, say: **"Soap** *starts with the sound /s/. Say* **ssssoap***."* After the student says ssssoap, say: *"Say /ssss/".* The student repeats the sound /ssss/.
- Point to the next picture in the row and name it. (Pictures are named on the *Recording and Scoring Form*.)
- Say: *"What is the first sound you hear in the word* (repeat the picture name)*?"*
- Repeat for the next two pictures and words.

Matching Final Phonemes - Use pictures at the top of *Student Page 3*.
- Demonstrate with the practice word **frog**:
  - Point to each of the four pictures as you say their names (listed on the *Recording and Scoring Form*) and have the student repeat the name of each picture.
  - Point to the picture of the frog and say: *"/g/ is the last sound in* **frog***. Say /g/."* After the student says /g/, say: *"Which picture here has the same last sound as* **frog***?"*
  - If the student points to the correct picture (pig), say: *"Yes,* **pig** *has the same last sound as* **frog***."*
  - If the student does not point to the correct picture (pig), say: **"Pig** *ends with the sound /g/, just like* **frog** *ends with the sound /g/. Say* **pig***, /g/.* (The student repeats.) *Say* **frog***, /g/."* (The student repeats.)
- Say: *"You do the next three by yourself. I'll tell you the names of the pictures. This is* (name the first picture)*."* (Pictures are named on the *Recording and Scoring Form*.)
- Point to and name the next three pictures. Say: *"Which one ends with the same sound as* (name the first picture in the row)*?"*
- Repeat for the next two words.

Identifying Final Phonemes - Use pictures in the last row on *Student Page 3*.
- Demonstrate with the practice word **cat**:
  - Point to the first picture and say: *"This is* **cat***. What is the last sound in the word* **cat***?"*
  - If the student correctly names the sound /t/, say: *"Yes, the last sound in* **cat** *is /t/."*
  - If the student does not name the sound /t/, say: **"Cat** *ends with the sound /t/. Say* **cat** *... /t/."* (The student repeats.)
- Point to the next picture in the row and name it using the word from the *Recording and Scoring Form*.
- Say, *"What is the last sound you hear in the word* (repeat the picture name)*?"*
- Repeat for the next two pictures and words.

Recording Instructions
- Put a check (√) next to the student's correct responses on the *Recording and Scoring Form*.
- Record any wrong answers the student gives, writing exactly what the student says in the space provided.
- If the student gives more than one response, write all attempts that are not correct.
- If the student self corrects, record all errors and note the self correction by writing "SC".
- If the student makes no attempt, write "NT" for "no try" next to the prompt on the *Recording and Scoring Form*.
- Write any observations about the student's responses or behavior in the Comment boxes on the *Recording and Scoring Form*.

Scoring Instructions
- After you finish giving the survey:
  - Record the number correct for each task in the Number Correct column.
  - Self corrections do not count as correct answers.
  - Total the number correct in the boxes in the Number Correct column.
  - Record the total correct at the bottom of the form.
  - Highlight or circle the appropriate skill level in the Skill Level boxes to the right of the Number Correct box.
- See User's Guide for more details about analyzing errors and interpreting results.

12

Phonological Awareness Survey   Recording and Scoring Form   Form A

Student _____ Grade _____ Age _____ Date _____

Assessor _____

	Record Student Response	Number Correct	Skill Level		
			Low	Emerging	Established
Compound Words use Student **page 1**		/3	0-1	2	3
practice: **rain** **bow**	*correct response:* **rainbow**	Comments:			
prompt: **cup** **cake** **sun** **shine** **cow** **boy**	cupcake sunshine cowboy				
2 Syllable Words use Student **page 1**		/3	0-1	2	3
prompt: **ta** **ble** **summ** **er** **con** **test**	*correct response:* table summer contest	Comments:			
Onset/Rime use Student **page 1**		/3	0-1	2	3
prompt: **/f/** **oot** **/p/** **art** **/sh/** **eep**	*correct response:* foot part sheep	Comments:			
Matching Initial Phonemes use Student **page 2**		/3	0-1	2	3
practice: *names of pictures, correct answers underlined* **moon** **pig** **ball** <u>**mouse**</u>		Comments:			
prompt: **socks** zebra <u>sun</u> fish **hat** pie monkey <u>horse</u> **car** ball goat <u>cat</u>					
Identifying Initial Phonemes use Student **page 2**		/3	0-1	2	3
practice: **soap**	*correct response:* **/s/**	Comments:			
prompt: **van** **top** **chain**	/v/ /t/ /ch/				
Matching Final Phonemes use Student **page 3**		/3	0-1	2	3
practice: *names of pictures, correct answers underlined* **frog** **cat** <u>**pig**</u> **sun**		Comments:			
prompt: **bat** <u>heart</u> man sled **horse** fan fish <u>bus</u> **key** bow apple <u>baby</u>					
Identifying Final Phonemes use Student **page 3**		/3	0 -1	2	3
practice: **cat**	*correct response:* **/t/**	Comments:			
prompt: **cab** **ram** **dish**	/b/ /m/ /sh/				
	Total	/21			

13

Phonological Awareness Survey

Student Page 1

Touch boxes for word parts.

Matching Beginning Sounds

Identifying Initial Phonemes

15

Phonological Awareness Survey

Student Page 3

Form A

Matching Final Sounds

Identifying Final Phonemes

16

Phonemic Awareness Survey

Summary Directions

More detailed directions are included in the *User's Guide*, available at www.ReallyGreatReading.com.

Instructions for Administering Survey
Put a check (√) on the *Recording and Scoring Form* next to any correct answers.
When the student makes an error, the assessor writes <u>exactly</u> what the student reads on the *Recording and Scoring Form.*
If the student does not attempt an answer, write "NT" for "no try".

<u>Blending 3 Phonemes</u> – Use the 3 boxes at the top of the *Student Page*.
- The teacher reads aloud the phonemes and the student names the word.
- Demonstrate with the practice word **mat**:
  - Say: ***"I am going to say 3 sounds. You put the sounds together and tell me the word. Let's practice together."***
  - Put the *Student Page* in front of the student.
  - Starting with the box on the student's left, touch each box on the *Student Page* as you say the sounds. Say: ***"The sounds are /m/*** (pause 1 second) ***/ă/*** (pause 1 second) ***/t/."***
  - Moving from the student's left to right, trace your finger under the boxes as you say the word *mat*. ***"When I put the sounds together, they make the word mat."***
  - Say: ***"Now you say the parts after I say them and touch the boxes as you say the parts."*** Touch the boxes as you say each sound and have the student touch the boxes as they say the sounds; ***"/m/*** (pause 1 second) ***/ă/*** (pause 1 second) ***/t/." "What is the word?"***
  - If the student gives the correct answer, continue with the sounds for the rest of the words.
  - If the student gives an incorrect answer say: ***"The sounds are /m/ /ă/ /t/ and the word is mat. You touch the boxes and say /m/ /ă/ /t/, mat."***
  - (If this is too difficult for the student, stop and give the Phonological Awareness Survey.)
- Say: ***"Let's do some more. You tell me what the word is."*** Read the sounds from the *Recording and Scoring Form* for the first word, pausing for one second between each sound. Then say: ***"What is the word?"***
- Repeat for the next two words.

<u>Segmenting 3 Phonemes</u> - Use the 3 boxes at the top of the *Student Page*.
- Teacher reads aloud a word and student names the phonemes in the word.
- Demonstrate with the practice word **seat**:
  - Say: ***"Now I am going say a word and you tell me the sounds. Let's practice one together. The word is seat."***
  - Starting with the box on the student's left, touch each box on the *Student Page* as you say the sounds; ***"The sounds in seat are /s/*** (pause 1 second) ***/ē/*** (pause 1 second) ***/t/."***
  - Say: ***"Now you tell me the sounds in seat."***
  - If the student gives the correct answer, continue with the rest of the words.
  - If the student gives an incorrect answer say: ***"The sounds in seat are /s/ /ē/ /t/. You touch the boxes and say /s/ /ē/ /t/, seat."***
  - (If this is too difficult for the student, stop and give the Phonological Awareness Survey.)
- Say: ***"Let's do some more. You tell me the sounds in*** (name first word on Recording and Scoring Form.)*"*** Read the first word from the *Recording and Scoring Form*.
- Repeat for the next two words on the *Recording and Scoring Form*.

17

<u>Blending 4 Phonemes</u> – Use the 4 boxes at the bottom of the *Student Page.*
- Say: ***"Now I am going to give you 4 sounds to blend into a word. You can use the 4 boxes at the bottom of the page to help."***
- Read the word from the *Recording and Scoring Form* and ask, ***"What is the word?"***
- Repeat for the second word.

<u>Segmenting 4 Phonemes</u> - Use the 4 boxes at the bottom of the *Student Page.*
   Say: ***"Now I am going say a word with 4 sounds. You tell me the sounds in the word. You can use the 4 boxes at the bottom of the page to help."***
- Read the sounds from the *Recording and Scoring Form* and ask, ***"What is the word?"***
- Repeat for the second word.

Recording Instructions
- Put a check (√) next to the student's correct responses on the *Recording and Scoring Form.*
- Record any wrong answers the student gives, writing <u>exactly</u> what the student says.
- If the student gives more than one response, write all attempts that are not correct.
- If student self corrects, record <u>all</u> errors and note the self correction by writing "SC".
- If the student makes no attempt, write "NT", for "no try" next to the prompt on the *Recording and Scoring Form.*
- Write any observations about what the student's reading and behaviors in the Comment boxes on the *Recording and Scoring Form.*

Scoring Instructions
- <u>After</u> you finish giving the survey:
  - Record the number correct for each task in the Number Correct column.
  - Total the number correct in the boxes in the Number Correct column and record the total at the bottom of the form.
  - Self corrections do <u>not</u> count as correct answers.
  - Highlight or circle the appropriate skill level in the skill level boxes to the right of the Number Correct box.
- See User's Guide for more details about analyzing errors and interpreting results.

18

Phonemic Awareness Survey	Recording and Scoring Form	Form A

Student _____ Grade _____ Age _____ Date _____

Assesor _____

	Record Student Response	Number Correct	Skill Level		
			Low	Emerging	Established
Blending 3 Phonemes use **top** of student page		/3	0-1	2	3

practice:		Comments:
prompt: /m/ /ă/ /t/	*response:* mat	
assessment:		
prompt:	*response:*	
/sh/ /ĭ/ /p/	ship	
/k/ /ō/ /t/	coat	
/d/ /ŭ/ /k/	duck	

Segmenting 3 Phonemes use **top** of student page		/3	0-1	2	3

practice:				Comments:
prompt: seat	*response:*	/s/	/ē/	/t/
assessment:				
prompt:	*response:*			
fit		/f/	/ĭ/	/t/
take		/t/	/ā/	/k/
sheep		/sh/	/ē/	/p/

Blending 4 Phonemes use **bottom** of student page		/2	0	1	2

assessment:		Comments:
prompt:	*response:*	
/b/ /ĕ/ /n/ /d/	bend	
/s/ /t/ /ō/ /n/	stone	

Segmenting 4 Phonemes use **bottom** of student page		/2	0	1	2

assessment:					Comments:
prompt:	*response:*				
belt	/b/	/ĕ/	/l/	/t/	
crab	/c/	/r/	/ă/	/b/	
			Totals	/10	

19

Phonemic Awareness Survey

Student Page

Touch boxes for sounds.

Appendix K: Grapheme Tile Templates

a	b	c	d	e	f
g	h	i	j	k	l
m	n	o	p	q	r
s	t	u	v	w	x
y	z	qu	ch	ng	sh

26	th	wh	ck	tch	dge
/ə/	ed	es	er	est	ing
se	ge	/d/	/t/	/ed/	♥
le	ff	ll	ss	zz	all
a-e	e-e	i-e	o-e	u-e	y-e
ai	au	augh	aw	ay	ea
ee	ei	eigh	ew	ey	ie
igh	oa	oe	oi	oo	ou
ough	ow	oy	ue	er	ir
ur	or	ar	ear	oar	ore

Appendix L: Glossary of Terms

Alphabetic Principle – The concept that in an alphabetic language, letters represent sounds and letter-sounds can be combined to form words.

Automaticity – The ability to read individual words quickly, accurately, and effortlessly. This is contrasted with fluency, which is the ability to read words in text accurately, quickly, and effortlessly with phrasing and intonation that reflects the meaning of the text.

Base Word – A word that has meaning when it stands by itself, to which suffixes and prefixes can be added. A compound word has two base words.

Blend – The process of combining word parts into a word: the two syllables *ta ble* can be blended into *table*. The phonemes /th/ /ŭ/ /m/ can be blended into *thumb*.

Closed Syllable – A syllable that has one vowel followed by one or more consonants. These patterns are closed syllables: vc *(at)*, cvc *(cat)*, ccvc *(chat)*, cvcc *(cash)*, ccvcc *(slash)*, cccvc *(strap)*, cccvcc *(shrimp)*, cccvccc *(springs)*, cvccc *(ranch)*, ccvccc *(trench)*. The vowel in a closed syllable is most often pronounced with its short sound.

Comprehension – The ability to understand what has been read. Comprehension is one of the five essential components of reading instruction identified in the Report of the National Reading Panel. The National Reading Panel concluded that a teacher's ability to demonstrate and teach an intentional, thoughtful interaction between the reader and the text improves comprehension. (*Report of the National Reading Panel*, 2000.)

Comprehension Monitoring – The mental act of knowing when a reader does and does not understand what is being read.

Consonant – A phoneme that is not a vowel. A consonant sound can be voiced or unvoiced. A consonant is formed with some obstruction of the flow of air by the lips, teeth, or tongue. Consonant sounds are /b/ /d/ /f/ /g/ /h/ /j/ /k/ /l/ /m/ /n/ /p/ /r/ /s/ /t/ /v/ /w/ /y/ /z/ /ch/ /sh/ /zh/ /ng/.

Content Word – Nouns, verbs, adjectives and adverbs. Content words carry the most meaning in a sentence, as contrasted with function words.

Continuant – Speech sound that can be spoken uninterruptedly until the speaker runs out of breath. Continuant sounds are /f/ /m/ /n/ /r/ /s/ /v/ /w/ /y/ /z/ /sh/ /zh/ /ng/. (The phonemes /y/ /w/ and /h/ are considered glides because they "glide" into the vowel that follows them. Linguists who do not classify these phonemes as glides differ as to whether these are categorized as stops or continuant phonemes.)

CVC – Consonant-vowel-consonant letter pattern in a word, which is one form of a closed syllable. A CVC word has a consonant, a vowel, and a consonant, in that order. The vowel in a CVC word is most often pronounced with its short sound. Examples of CVC words are *bat, yes, him, cop,* and *run*.

Decodable Materials – Sentences, paragraphs or stories in which a large proportion of words (generally 95% or more) comprise letters-sound relationships that have already been taught and sight words already taught. Decodable materials are used to provide practice with specific decoding skills and to help students apply the phonics lessons that have been taught.

Decoding – The process of translating a word from speech to print, usually using knowledge of letter-sound relationships. Also, the act of deciphering an unknown or unfamiliar word by sounding it out.

DIBELS – *Dynamic Indicators of Early Literacy Skills.* Screening assessments for literacy skills in grades K through 6.

Digraph – Two letters that together represent one consonant sound. The most common digraphs are ch (*chin*), sh (*shape*), th (*thumb* or *this*), wh (*white*), ph (*phone*), ng (*string*), gh (*tough*), ck (*duck*).

Diphthong – Vowel sounds that have a glide and may feel as if they have two parts. The most obvious diphthongs are /ow/ as in *house* and /oi/ as in *oil*.

Dry-Erase Board – A board of any size that easily erases when dry-erase markers are used.

Elkonin Boxes – Adjacent boxes on a piece of paper or card that are used for placing tokens or letters that represent sounds. Named for a Russian psychologist who first used the boxes for this purpose.

Encoding – The process of spelling a word, usually using knowledge of letter-sound relationships.

Expository Text – Text that reports factual information.

Flash Word – High frequency words that are spelled using phonetic sound-symbol relationships that have been taught. These words can be read phonetically, but they have to be read and spelled "in a flash" because they occur so often in print.

Fluency – One of the five essential components of reading instruction, according to the National Reading Panel. Fluency is measured as a reading rate, most often as the words read correctly in one minute. A part of fluency that is not objectively measurable is prosody, which is using the correct intonation when reading to reflect the meaning of the text. Accuracy is another critical component of fluency that is not often explicitly measured, the explicit measure being correct words read as a percent of total words read. (Accuracy is only implicitly considered when calculating words correct per minute.)

Function Word – These include articles, conjunctions, prepositions, pronouns, and auxiliary words. These are not content words.

Glide – A consonant phoneme that glides immediately into a vowel. Examples are /y/ as in *yes* and /w/ as in *wind*. The /y/ and /w/ sounds cannot be precisely separated from the vowel sound that follows. /h/ as in *hat* is also sometimes considered a glide.

Grapheme – Letter or letters that represents a phoneme in a word. The word *dough* has two phonemes, /d/ and /ō/, and two graphemes, *d* and *ough*.

Guide Word – A word used to help a student remember a sound. The guide words for the short vowel letter-sound matches used in *Teaching Reading Essentials* demonstration lessons on short vowel sounds are: ă – apple, ĕ – edge, ĭ – itch, ŏ – octopus, ŭ – up.

Heart Words – High frequency words that are not spelled with phonetic rules that have been taught. These words have to be "learned by heart". An example of a heart word is said — the sounds are /s/ /ĕ/ /d/. The expected spelling is s-e-d, but the actual spelling is s-a-i-d. The "ai" portion of the word has to be "learned by heart."

Inflectional Suffix – A suffix that combines with base words to indicate tense (*walking*, *walked*), or number (*rats*, *churches*), comparison (*faster*, *fastest*), or possession (*hers*). Inflectional suffixes do not change the word's part of speech.

Long Vowel – A term used to denote a vowel sound that is spoken with tension in the vocal cords. The long vowel sounds used in the *Teaching Reading Essentials* lessons have the same sound as a letter name: these are /ā/ as in *make*, /ē/ as in *Pete*, /ī/ as in *kite*, /ō/ as in *bone*, and /ū/ as in *cube*.

Magic *e* – see Silent *e*.

Magnetic Receptive – Capable of holding material that is magnetized. A magnetic receptive dry-erase board is made of a metal that will hold magnetized materials and has a surface from which marks made with dry-erase markers are easily erased.

Morpheme – The smallest meaningful unit of language. Roots, base words, suffixes, prefixes, and combining forms are all morphemes. The word *basketball* has two morphemes: <u>basket</u> and <u>ball</u>. The word *inspector* has three morphemes: <u>in spect or</u>. The word *walking* has two morphemes: <u>walk</u> and <u>ing.</u> The word *unwillingly* has four morphemes: <u>un will ing ly</u>. The word *thermometer* has two morphemes: <u>thermo</u> and <u>meter</u>.

National Reading Panel – Fourteen educators and educational scholars who assessed the status of research-based knowledge about the effectiveness of various approaches to teaching reading. The panel published the results of its meta-analysis in *The Report of the National Reading Panel* in 2000, which can be found at http://www.nationalreadingpanel.org.

Nonsense Word – A word that does not have meaning in the English language. Nonsense words are sometimes called "make believe words." In *Teaching Reading Essentials* lessons, they are called Martian words because they are words we might hear Martians use. We can read and spell nonsense words, but we don't know what they mean.

Onset – The part of a syllable before the vowel. In the word *shrimp*, <u>shr</u> is the onset. Not all words have onsets. For example, the words *I, oak,* and *ice* do not have onsets.

Orthography – A writing system. Includes the rules governing the spelling in an alphabetic writing system such as English.

Phoneme – The smallest unit of sound in a word. Phonemes are combined in a language system to make words.

Phoneme Awareness – The conscious awareness that words are made of phonemes and that the phonemes are represented by letters in the English orthographic system. A person with phoneme awareness can identify, remember, and manipulate phonemes in words.

Phonics – Study of the relationship between sounds and letters. Also, the system of instruction that teaches the relationship between sounds and letters.

Phonological Awareness – Conscious awareness of all levels of the speech sound system, including pronouncing words, remembering names and lists, identifying syllables, blending and segmenting syllables into words, creating rhymes, detecting syllable stress, and blending and segmenting phonemes into words. Phoneme Awareness is a sub-category of Phonological Awareness.

Prefix – A morpheme that that is attached to the front of a root or base word and that modifies or contributes to the word's meaning.

Prosody – Reading with pace, rhythm, and intonation that supports the meaning of the text.

R-controlled Vowel – A vowel that is immediately followed by the letter *r*. The vowel's pronunciation is affected by the *r*, and often the vowel is combined with the *r* so that together the vowel and the *r* spell one phoneme (*bird, turn, herd* are examples).

Rime – The part of a syllable that includes the vowel and everything after it. In the word *shrimp*, *imp* is the rime. A rime may include only the vowel. For example, in the word *toe*, the rime is *oe*. The rime is the part of a word that sounds the same as another word when words rhyme.

Root – A morpheme that cannot stand alone and is often used in a family of words with related meanings. "Spect" is the root in these words: *inspect, respect, spectacle, prospect, spectator*. A root is usually of Latin origin in English words.

Schwa – An almost indistinct vowel sound found in unstressed syllables in English. The schwa sound is represented by the symbol /ə/. Examples of the schwa sound are *salad* and *wagon*. (The schwa sound is represented by the underlined letter.)

Screening Assessment – Assessments given to provide information about an individual student's skills with regard to a particular subject. DIBELS benchmark assessments are screening assessments for reading, as is the Texas Primary Reading Inventory (TPRI) and Phonological Awareness Literacy Screening (PALS).

Segment – To break into parts. The word *napkin* can be segmented into syllables: *nap kin*. The word *chat* can be segmented into phonemes: /ch/ /ă/ /t/.

Short Vowel – A term used to denote a vowel sound that is spoken with lax vocal cords. The short vowel sounds used in the *Teaching Reading Essentials* lessons are /ă/ as in *apple*, /ĕ/ as in *echo*, /ĭ/ as in *itch*, /ŏ/ as in *octopus*, and /ŭ/ as in *up*.

Sight Words – Words that are recognized as wholes and do not have to be sounded out. This term often refers to words that are high frequency words and do not follow common phonetic patterns.

Silent *e* – The silent *e* at the end of a VC*e* word that works with the first vowel to represent a long vowel sound. Silent *e* is also called super *e* or magic *e*.

Sound Box – Informal name for the two slash marks that enclose a letter or letters to indicate a sound, not a letter name. For example, /b/ indicates the first sound in the word *boat*, not the name of the letter *b*. The /k/ sound represents the sound /k/ whether it is spelled with a *c* as in *cat*, a *k* as in *kite*, or a *ck* as in *duck*.

Sound Chain – A list of words in which one sound changes from word to word, resulting in one colored letter tile changing in the word. An example of a sound chain is: *rate, great, greet, green, grin, grim, rim, rhyme, time, type, tip, sip.* Students do not spell words in sound chains, they represent the sounds with colored tiles or other markers.

Stop – Consonant speech sound that is articulated with a stop of the air stream creating the sound. Stop sounds are /p/ /b/ /t/ /d/ /ch/ /j/ /k/ /g/.

Stressed Syllable – An accented syllable in a multisyllable word articulated with greater loudness or stress.

Stretching Sounds – Occurs when a person extends one finger while articulating each sound in a word. The word *bat* requires three fingers to "stretch the sounds" /b/ /ă/ /t/, as would the word *chin*, /ch/ /ĭ/ /n/. The word *club* would use four fingers to "stretch the sounds" /k/ /l/ /ŭ/ /b/.

Suffix – A letter or group of letters that when added to a root or base word that changes the word's part of speech or modifies its meaning.

Super *e* – See Silent *e.*

Syllable – A unit of pronunciation organized around a vowel. A syllable can be only one vowel sound (the word *I*), it can have as many as three consonant sounds before or after the vowel (the words *scrap* and *tempt*, respectively), or it can begin or end with a vowel (*ape* and *pie*, respectively).

Syllable Board – A piece of laminated material on which the student can write word parts with a dry erase marker. The syllable boards used in *Teaching Reading Essentials* are from Really Great Reading Company (www.reallygreatreading.com). Teachers can also make syllable boards at a very reasonable cost from bathroom laminate that can be purchased from hardware or stores. Two other ways to make syllable strips are by laminating card stock and cutting it into 3" x 5" pieces or cutting up purchased dry-erase sentence strips.

Syntax – Rules governing the arrangement of words in sentences.

Touch and Say – A multisensory activity where the student touches each letter tile spelling a word while saying the sound represented by the letter tile. The student then runs his or her finger under the word, from left to right, and reads the word.

Vocabulary – One of the five essential components of reading, according to the National Reading Panel. The National Reading Panel found many ways to effectively improve a student's vocabulary. (*Report of the National Reading Panel*, 2000.)

Voiced Sounds – Speech sounds articulated with vibrating vocal cords. All vowel sounds are voiced. Voiced consonant sounds are /b/ /d/ /g/ / /j/ /l/ /m/ /n/ /r/ /v/ /w/ /y/ /z/ /zh/.

Vowel – A phoneme that is articulated with no blockage of the air flow. Every syllable has a vowel sound. The English language has 16 vowel sounds, which are /ē/ as in *eagle*, /ĭ/ as in *itch*, /ā/ as in *ape*, /ĕ/ as in *echo*, /ă/ as in *apple*, /ī/ as in *ice*, /ŏ/ as in *octopus*, /ŭ/ as in *up*, /aw/ as in *awful*, /ō/ as in *ocean*, /ŏŏ/ as in *foot*, /ōō/ as in *school*, /ə/ as in *wagon*, /oi/ as in *boil*, and /ou/ as in *out*, and /er/ as in *her*. When teaching reading, we also classify /ar/ and /or/ as r-controlled vowel sounds, although these are not always classified as vowels by linguists.

VC – Vowel-consonant letter pattern in a word, also one form of a closed syllable. A VC word has one vowel followed by one consonant. Examples of VC words are *on, at, it, ed,* and *up.*

VC*e* – Vowel-consonant-*e* letter pattern in a syllable. The first vowel is usually long, and the *e* is silent. A VC*e* word has a vowel, a consonant and an *e*. The *e* at the end of the word works with the vowel before the consonant to represent the long vowel sound of the first vowel. Examples of VC*e* words are *slime, ape, Pete, cone,* and *tube.*

Vowel Team – A vowel spelling, or grapheme, that uses two or more letters to spell a vowel sound. *Oa, ow, oe,* and *ough* are four vowel teams that spell the long *o* sound.

Unvoiced Sounds – Sounds spoken with no vibration of the vocal cords. Unvoiced sounds are: /f/ /h/ /k/ /p/ /s/ /t/ /ch/ /sh/.

Word Chain – A list of words in which one sound changes from word to word, resulting in one letter tile changing in the word. An example of a word chain is: *bat, ban, fan, fin, fish, dish, dash, mash, rash, trash, trap.* (The words with the /sh/ sound can be included in the word chain because /sh/ is spelled with the letters sh, which are on one letter tile.)